lo

POCKET
LOS ANGELES

Ryan Ver Berkmoes

Contents

Plan Your Trip   4

The Journey Begins Here 4
Our Picks 6
Perfect Days 22
Get Prepared 26
When To Go 28
Getting There 30
Getting Around 31
A Few Surprises 34

**Top: Delicious cheeseburgers
Bottom: Downtown LA (p53)**

Explore Los Angeles 37

Hollywood 39
Downtown 53
Griffith Park, Los Feliz & Echo Park 71
Exposition Park & South LA 85
Pasadena & Highland Park 95
Koreatown, Miracle Mile & Mid-City ... 107
West Hollywood & Beverly Hills 121
Santa Monica 133
Venice & South Coast Beaches 145
Burbank & Universal City 155

Los Angeles Toolkit 169

Family Travel 170
Accommodations 171
Food, Drink & Nightlife 172
LGBTQ+ Travelers 174
Health & Safe Travel 175
Responsible Travel 176
Accessible Travel 178
Nuts & Bolts 179
Index 180

★ Top Experiences

Hollywood Boulevard 44
The Hollywood Sign 46
The Broad 60
Walt Disney Concert Hall 62
Griffith Park 76
Griffith Observatory 78
Exposition Park 90
The Huntington 100
The New LACMA 112
Academy Museum
of Motion Pictures 113
Petersen Automotive
Museum 114
Santa Monica Pier 138
Venice's Beach & Boardwalk 150
Universal Studios Hollywood 158

The Journey Begins Here

When I was a teenager, I ditched my family at the Original Farmers Market and snuck into the neighboring CBS Television City, where I watched Carol Burnett rehearse her hysterical Saturday night show. My fascination with all things LA has never waned. From tracking down obscure movie locations from the prescient 1956 *Invasion of the Body Snatchers* to getting the best-ever tour of Warner Bros with a friend who works there, the city is always a thrill. Finding the best doughnut, picking the perfect street taco, going on a neighborhood walk – I never tire of exploring LA.

Ryan Ver Berkmoes
Bluesky @ryanvb
Ryan is a proudly native-born Californian and has researched and written more than 170 Lonely Planet guidebooks.

Hollywood Boulevard (p44)
SEAN PAVONE/SHUTTERSTOCK

THE BEST

Dining Experiences

LA dining is a global feast. There's no shortage of just-like-the-homeland dishes, from *xiao long bao* (noodles) to *pupusas* (savory-filled dough) to waffles. Add in California's farmland bounty and you'll chew your way through your visit.

Grab a lunch seat at **Sushi Gen** in Little Tokyo; chefs carve slabs of the freshest fish. Dinner is less frenetic. (p66)

Enjoy modern takes on Middle Eastern classics from across the region at sleek, loud **Bavel**. It's showered in cascading vines. (p66)

Indulge in the ultimate LA experience at fine-dining **Providence**: fine seafood, stellar service, stunt-free cuisine. (p50; pictured above)

Grab a meal or snack any time of day at the **Original Farmers Market**, an open-air 1934 landmark. (p115; pictured above)

Create your first or last memory of LA, going to/from LAX, at **Randy's Donuts**. The simplest, like the glazed old-fashioned, are best. (p93)

Assemble a picnic at hyperlocal bakery, cafe and deli **Gjusta**. Great patio; sits behind a nondescript storefront. (p152)

Right: Randy's Donuts (p93)

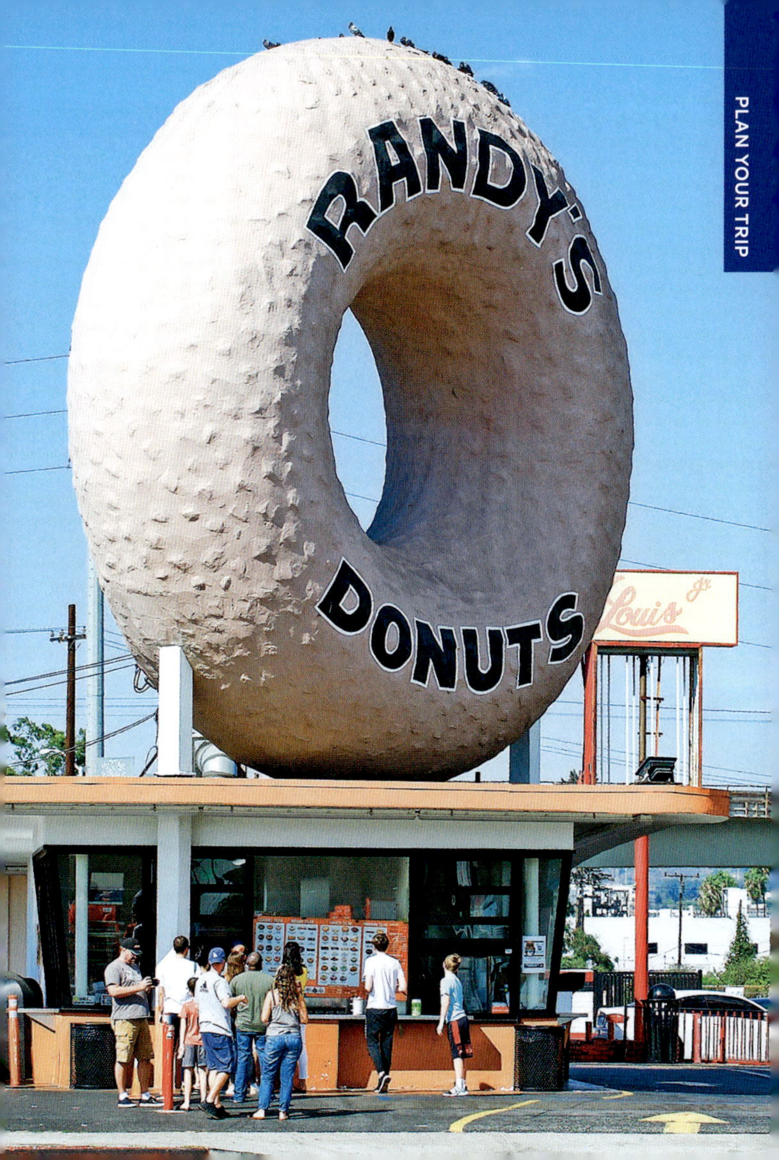
RANDY'S
DONUTS
Louis Jr

THE BEST

Bar Experiences

From postindustrial coffee roasters to mid-century stalwarts and from classic Hollywood martini bars to cocktail-pouring rooftop lounges, LA serves its drinks with a generous splash of wow.

Move amid an industry-heavy crowd at loud, dimly lit **El Carmen**, festooned with bull heads and *lucha libre* (Mexican wrestling) memorabilia. (p119)

Enjoy classic lounge acts nightly at the **Dresden**, an old-school bar-restaurant with moodily lit rooms and red-wine-colored booths. (p80; pictured above)

Patronise a true Hollywood dive at **Frolic Room**, which has served everyone from Judy Garland to Charles Bukowski. Great sign. (p51)

Choose from speakeasy downstairs and cool bar upstairs at **Townhouse & Del Monte Speakeasy**; its history goes back to 1915. (p153)

Join hipsters, surfers and shamblers at **Waterfront**, an indoor-outdoor beach bar ideally suited to the Venice Boardwalk. (p153; pictured above)

Look for the neon sign in Koreatown: **Lock & Key** is a classy lounge with a cool dance patio. (p119)

Right: Frolic Room (p51)

THE BEST

Responsible Travel Experiences

Los Angeles offers many responsible and sustainable experiences. Generally, it's a forward-thinking place, so feel-good times start with positive energy. With environmental laws in place, further green practices abound.

Don't miss LA's markets, stocked with organic produce, flowers, baked goods and prepared foods. Among the best are the **Santa Monica Farmers Markets**, especially on Wednesday, when famous chefs come hunting. (p140)

Engage with the Holocaust, the life of Anne Frank and disinformation at the **Museum of Tolerance**. Learning the hard lessons of humanity's past so they aren't repeated is at the core of the museum's mission. (p126; pictured above)

See LA's history through the filters of poverty, women's suffrage and civil rights at the heartfelt **Museum of Social Justice**. Exhibits change regularly. (p64; pictured above)

Tour LA's world-famous beaches along the 22-mile **Marvin Braude Bike Trail**. The paved coastal path starts in Santa Monica and ends at Torrance Beach. (p139)

Right: Marvin Braude Bike Trail (p139)

Treasure Hunt Experiences

Los Angeles is a pro at luring cards out of wallets. After all, how could you not bag that supercute vintage-fabric dress or that tongue-in-cheek tote? You can shop for anything in this town.

Browse cluttered, old-school **Larry Edmunds Bookshop** for new and used entertainment industry books. (p49)

Run your eye over custom boards, gear and art exhibits at **Kingswell**, one of SoCal's best skate shops. Has its own line of clothing. (p83; pictured above)

Tap the source for eclectic LA-based fiction at **Book Soup**, a great indie bookstore with thoughtful staff recs. (p129)

Take advantage of Oskar de la Cruz' sharp eye for rare vintage threads at **Luxe De Ville**. (p83; pictured above)

See the vision of rapper Tyler, the Creator, known for his alternative hip-hop, at his clothing store **Golf Wang**. (p119)

Search for a gem at industry legend **It's a Wrap!**, an outlet used to unload on-screen wardrobes and props. Great prices on designer labels. (p161)

Right: Book Soup (p129)

PLAN YOUR TRIP

OUR PICKS

NORTHSKY FILMS/SHUTTERSTOCK

Skate park, Venice (p150)

THE BEST

Active LA Experiences

After being jammed in traffic, Angelenos love to get physical. Theirs is a city made for pace-quickening thrills, with spectacular mountain hikes and one of the country's largest urban parks.

Start your explorations of Griffith Park with the family-friendly jaunt up **Bronson Canyon**, a popular shooting location. With more than 50 miles of trails, the park is LA's hub of hiking. (p76)

Get up close and personal with the iconic 50ft-tall letters of the **Hollywood Sign** on hikes over three great trails. (p46; pictured above)

See Hollywood, Beverly Hills and greater LA on highly recommended tours with **Bikes & Hikes LA**. Its signature ride is the 32-mile 'LA in a Day,' which takes in everything. (p126)

Witness a world-class spectacle at Venice Beach's public, ocean-view **skate park**. It's a destination for both high flyers and those who simply want to stand and admire, in the region where the sport was invented. (p150)

THE BEST

Live Music Experiences

Much of the recording industry is based in LA, and the abundance of world-class musicians, paired with spectacular and historic venues, makes it essential to enjoy a live performance.

Be entertained under the stars by top headliners at the **Hollywood Bowl**. It hosted its first concert in 1922. (p47)

See where the Doors were the house band back in the '60s at Sunset Blvd's legendary **Whisky-a-Go-Go**. (p127)

Head downstairs at crowded dive bar **Echo** to its alt bar, Echoplex, known for punk rock and other styles. (p80)

Explore the **Los Angeles Music Center**, one of the largest performing arts complexes in the USA, with venues such as the Walt Disney Concert Hall. (p62)

Get close to the acts at the **Roxy Theatre** on Sunset Strip. (p127)

Whisky-a-Go-Go (p127)

ALEX MILLAUER/SHUTTERSTOCK

SIMON URWIN/LONELY PLANET

Will Rogers State Beach (p137)

THE BEST

Beach Experiences

With miles and miles of wide, sandy coastline, beach life and surf culture are part of the freewheeling SoCal lifestyle, so come out and play and hit the waves.

Admire sandstone rock towers rising from emerald coves at **El Matador State Beach**. Dolphins breach the surface beyond the waves. (p143)

Join large groups of migratory birds at **Malibu Lagoon State Beach**. North are popular surf breaks. (p143)

See where *Baywatch* was shot at **Will Rogers State Beach**, lined with volleyball courts. (p137)

Look for the **Original Muscle Beach**, south of Santa Monica Pier, where Southern California's exercise craze began in the 1930s and '40s. (p137)

Prepare for sensory overload at **Venice Beach**, one of LA's essential experiences. Many colorful people come together here. (p150)

Visit the cradle of beach volleyball. **Manhattan Beach** may have gone chic, but its salty-dog heart still beats. (p151)

THE BEST

Celebrity-Spotting Experiences

Admit it: you want to see a celeb. Don't apologize. Maybe it's the talent, or thinking some stardust will rub off. Or maybe, just maybe, you'll get the selfie...

Beeline for buzzing **Grandmaster Recorders**, once home to the namesake recording studio. Its rooftop bar and dining area with Hollywood vistas attracts famous names. (p50)

Pay homage to dearly departed icons at **Hollywood Forever Cemetery**, filled with vainglorious tombstones and epic mausoleums. (p48)

Enjoy martinis and high-end burgers with sublime views at old-school **Tower Bar**. It's Hollywood luxury packaged at the swank Sunset Tower Hotel. (p128)

Dress up and swill martinis at the Beverly Hills Hotel's legendary **Polo Lounge**. Movie studio titans really do still hammer out deals at the tables while celebs huddle with agents. (p129)

Hollywood Forever Cemetery (p48)

TIM RICHARDS/LONELY PLANET

COURTESY OF CALIFORNIA STATE PARKS, 2025

Watts Towers (p92)

THE BEST

Under-the-Radar Experiences

With so much diversity and life in such a huge package, you could say that most of LA is under the radar. Certainly, it's far richer than its celeb-centric image.

Head to the busy **Piñata District** for the ultimate in colorful art. High-ceilinged emporiums display legions of aliens and other characters waiting to spew forth candy. (p65)

Marvel at the triple spires of the fabulous **Watts Towers**, which rank among the world's greatest monuments of folk art. In 1921 Italian immigrant Simon Rodia set out to 'make something big,' and did. (p92)

Get the full background on LA's original Chinatown at the **Chinese American Museum**. In the 1930s LA's powerful conspired to tear down the neighborhood because it was too close to City Hall. (p58)

Visit the **Breed Street Shul Project**, which is restoring a 1922 Byzantine Revival synagogue. The neighborhood once had the largest Jewish population west of Chicago. (p69)

THE BEST

LGBTQ+ Experiences

The rainbow flag flies highest along Santa Monica Blvd in West Hollywood (WeHo), one of the top LGBTQ+ neighborhoods in the US. Less-vaunted scenes are found in Silver Lake and throughout LA.

Visit one of the most iconic gay nightclubs on the West Coast, the **Abbey**. It's as much a community center as a bar and club. (p126)

Get your Sunday afternoon brunch on at **Hamburger Mary's**, the go-to in WeHo. The only problem with brunch in WeHo is that eventually it's Monday. (p126)

Join the near-permanent party along Santa Monica Blvd in WeHo. Choices include the iconic **Micky's Weho**, with long-running drag shows and great DJ sets. (p126)

People-watch at Silver Lake's **Black Cat**, the site of a 1967 LGBTQ+ civil rights demonstration after a police raid on New Year's Eve. Today it's still a neighborhood hangout. (p81)

The Abbey (p126)

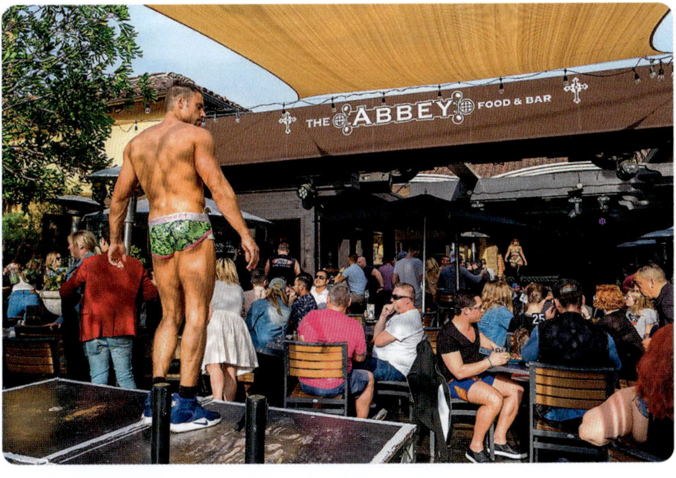

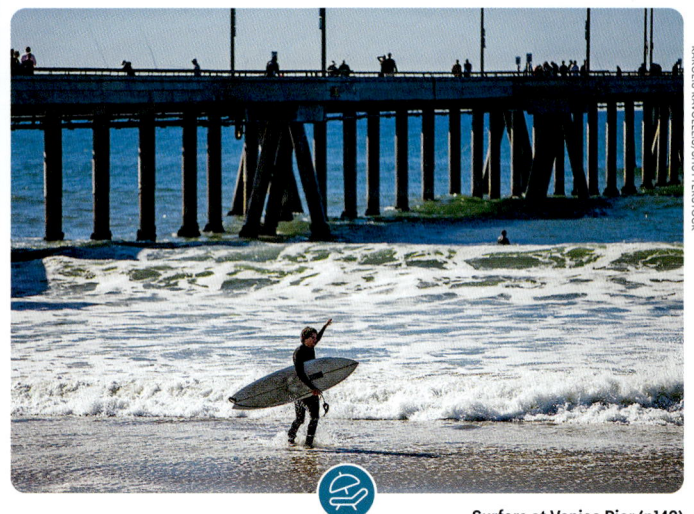

Surfers at Venice Pier (p149)

THE BEST

Laid-Back LA Experiences

Take a moment to live the LA life at these places that embody the easy-living lifestyle of the clichés, where every day's a beach and cares are for other people.

Have lunch on the sand near the pier at semi-private **Paradise Cove**, the setting for *The Rockford Files*. (p143)

Don't miss the deep-fried treats at **Donut Friend**, sprinkled with coconut bacon or made with bananas. (p103)

Sit on the welcoming patio at **Venice Ale House**, at Venice's northern end, for sunset people-watching and good tunes. (p152)

Choose upstairs cantina **Bar Flores** for a long evening with friends. Facing Sunset Blvd, it has a candlelit glow and a mellow vibe. (p82)

Enjoy tacos and platters at **Teddy's Red Tacos**. It does the long-simmered, piquant Mexican stew *birria* better than nearly anyone. (p152)

Experience the quieter end of Venice Beach at **Venice Pier**. The commercial strip and associated mania are north. (p149)

Best for Kids

Admire Santa Monica Pier's most compelling landmark, **Pacific Park**. Every angle is dominated by family-friendly arcades, carnival games, the soaring Ferris wheel and tame roller coaster. (p138)

———————————————

Tour a striking ode to the auto at the **Petersen Automotive Museum**, with an entire area devoted to the drivers of tomorrow. (p114)

———————————————

Take young engineers to ride the rails for a modest fare on **three pint-sized railroads** circling Griffith Park's perimeter. (p76)

———————————————

Learn about paleontology at the **La Brea Tar Pits & Museum**. Mammoths and other critters roamed LA's savanna in prehistoric times, sometimes coming to a sticky end. (p115)

———————————————

Visit the definitive kid-friendly attraction at **Universal Studios Hollywood**. Rides are themed to Harry Potter, The Simpsons, Jurassic World, Super Nintendo World and various Universal properties. (p158)

Best for Free

Feast on art, design and botanical beauty at the palatial **Getty Center**, straddling a hilltop in the Santa Monica Mountains. (p130)

———————————————

Take in more than 2000 postwar pieces at **The Broad**. Artists represented include Cindy Sherman, Jeff Koons, Andy Warhol, Roy Lichtenstein and Kara Walker. (p60)

———————————————

Focus on works created from the 1940s to the present at **MOCA**. There's no shortage of work by luminaries, among them Mark Rothko and David Hockney. (p63)

———————————————

Gaze down at LA from the 27th-floor observation deck at **Los Angeles City Hall**, the 1928 phallic-shaped star of *Dragnet, LA Confidential* and countless other shows. (p63)

———————————————

Educate yourself on the African American experience in California and LA at **CAAM** (California African American Museum), showcasing works by African American artists. (p91)

Perfect Days

Pick a neighborhood from the many LA has to offer and then set out for a great day in the City of Angels, maybe pausing for a famous doughnut along the way.

TCL Chinese Theatre, Hollywood (p45)

DAY ONE

Only Have One Day?

MORNING

Walk all over your favorite stars on the **Hollywood Walk of Fame** (p44) and size up their handprints outside **TCL Chinese Theatre** (p44).

AFTERNOON

Hasten over to the **Original Farmers Market** (p115) and graze your way to a fresh and wonderful lunch. Just south, dig into movie magic at the extraordinary **Academy Museum of Motion Pictures** (p113; pictured above). Next door, get a dose of fine art in the striking new building at **LACMA** (p112).

EVENING

After dinner at historic old Hollywood **Musso & Frank Grill** (p50), round your day out with live comedy at the **Laugh Factory** (p127) or **Improv** (p117).

◼ DAY TWO ◼

A Weekend Trip

MORNING

Explore Downtown LA (DTLA), reserving tickets in advance for the spectacular modern art at **The Broad** (p60) and exploring the city's Spanish heritage at **El Pueblo de Los Ángeles** (p64).

AFTERNOON

Following lunch at **Grand Central Market** (p63; pictured above), explore **Little Tokyo** (p64) and walk the busy streets of **Chinatown** (p58). Browse the galleries and shops in the **Arts District** (p65) and **Row DTLA** (p67).

EVENING

Have cocktails at **Everson Royce Bar** (p67) and then a sublime, modern meal at **Bavel** (p66). Enjoy an evening of music in the great acoustics of **Walt Disney Concert Hall** (p62); book tickets in advance.

◼ DAY THREE ◼

A Short Break

MORNING

Use your pre-booked admission at the **Getty Center** (p130; pictured above), a spectacular synergy of art, architecture, landscaping and panoramic views.

AFTERNOON

Have lunch at innovative, produce-driven **Gjusta** (p152) in eclectic **Venice** (p145). Satiated, hunt down unique fashion, accessories and art along **Abbot Kinney Boulevard** (p151), then stroll, pedal or in-line skate along the **boardwalk** (p150), taking in its street art, nutty souvenirs and acres of powdery sand.

EVENING

Wrap up the day in neighboring **Santa Monica** (p133), catching a perfect SoCal sunset from its **pier** (p138), before heading up the coast to dinner with a view at **Nobu Malibu** (p142).

If You Have More Time

Roll things out with a **Warner Bros Studio Tour** (p160), visiting backlot sets and technical departments and eyeing up some of Hollywood's most famous soundstages. If you prefer theme-park rides, opt for nearby **Universal Studios Hollywood** (p158).

Drop by **Exposition Park** (p90) for three impressive museums, all surrounding a world-class **rose garden** (p88). See what's on at **CAAM** (California African American Museum; p91), which has ever-changing exhibits by top artists and photographers. Then get wowed at the nearby **California Science Center** (p90) and see dinosaurs at the **Natural History Museum** (p90).

Head up to the landmark **Griffith Observatory** (p78) in time to watch the sun sink over the city. Afterwards, head down toward Echo Park and, assuming you got your tickets well ahead, go see LA's much-loved **Dodgers** (p79) play at Dodger Stadium near Echo Park. Have a Dodger Dog in the park.

Warner Bros Studios complex (p160)

WALTER CICCHETTI/SHUTTERSTOCK

A City Day Trip

Top of the list for many LA visitors is a trip to **Disneyland® Resort** (p162; pictured above). Located down south in Anaheim, it's an easy day trip.

To make the most of your day – and Disneyland®'s significant cost – you'll want to get an early start. If driving, the morning rush-hour traffic is unavoidable for the first part of the 25-mile drive. Alternatively, taking Metrolink or Amtrak will allow you to enjoy the ride and breakfast on the train.

Take your time, enjoy Disneyland® Park (the proper name for the original park) and Disney California Adventure. Have dinner, then (post traffic) head back to LA.

On a Rainy Day

When the skies open up in LA, you're in luck! Four of the top attractions are a puddle splash from each other. Start at the **La Brea Tar Pits & Museum** (p115; pictured above). Enjoy the museum, then sniff out the tar pits on the short walk next door to spectacular **LACMA** (p112) and its radical new art displays.

Your next stop is another splash away. The **Academy Museum of Motion Pictures** (p113) can easily fill half your day. Save time for the **Petersen Automotive Museum** (p114) right across Wilshire Blvd. The Academy museum and LACMA both have good food options.

Get Prepared

Stay Cool

Los Angeles is a sprawling place made up of people from all over the world and the US. Even so, different parts of LA vary widely in culture. One cliché of the city, the laid-back 'it's cool, man' persona, comes from the necessity of getting along in a place where everybody has a different set of customs and habits. It's an attitude that lets each person get by.

Walk LA

Los Angeles is dotted with walkable neighborhoods. A few examples:
Downtown History, architecture and classic movie backdrops.
Echo Park Great, historic park and neighborhood.
Highland Park Figueroa St is a thriving strip.
West Hollywood Sunset Blvd is dotted with icons and surprises.
Mid-City Wilshire Blvd is lined with cultural powerhouses; Melrose Blvd is the storied land of offbeat boutiques.
Venice Walk the beach, canals and Abbot Kinney Blvd.

Things to Know

Beaches Virtually all Californian beaches are open to the public. Even if access appears to be blocked by gated enclaves, the sands are yours to enjoy. There'll always be nearby, marked public access points.
Griffith Park You don't have to go all the way to the beach for the kids to have fun outside. Griffith Park is huge and filled with attractions, from train rides to hiking to the famous observatory.
Eat local LA is awash in great locally owned eateries. Some of the best are food trucks, run with passionate care by cooks who deliver superb meals for the lowest possible prices. For mouthwatering reviews of legendary Cal-Mex street food, check out **LA Taco** (lataco.com).

TIPPING

Tipping is not optional: it's part of the workers' wages.

15–20%

Bartenders
Always. Per round, minimum $2 per drink.

$2–4

Housekeeping staff
Always, daily.

$2–5

Parking valets
Always, when your car is returned.

20–25%

Restaurant servers
Always, of the total bill.

DAILY BUDGET

BUDGET: Less than $150
- Dorm bed: $35–75
- Takeout meal: $8–15
- Free concerts and events
- Metro daily fare cap: $5

MIDRANGE: $150–350
- Hotel double room: $200
- Two-course dinner and a drink: $50
- Museum for two: $40
- Metro plus rideshare: $30

TOP END: More than $350
- Beach or West Hollywood hotel: from $300
- Dinner at top-end restaurant: from $200
- Big-name concert: $100
- All rideshare transportation: $100

Currency
US dollar ($)

Language
English (with a lot of Spanish)

Time
Pacific Time (GMT/UTC minus eight hours)

TIP

The top mistake first-timers to LA make is misjudging the amount of time they need to navigate this vast, sprawling place. It needs repeating often: plan your days for one area only.

When to Go

LA's so big that it's hard for an event to be as big as the city, but some come close.

Winter is the wettest season and temperatures are generally mild. But don't go getting the parka out. Cold here is temperate elsewhere. Spring is the ideal time to visit. Rainfall drops dramatically by April and those mild temps are verging on balmy. Aesthetically, the hills are enjoying their brief period of green-hued glory, accented by splashes of wildflowers.

Summer is indeed peak tourist season, with hot weather and big crowds. The beaches are at their best. Autumn rivals spring, but the scenery has been baked brown and the fire danger is high.

The Big Events

January Pasadena celebrates the New Year with the **Tournament of Roses Parade** (p102), the world-class spectacle of sweet-smelling floats and much more.

May **Cinco de Mayo** celebrates the Mexican victory over the French at the Battle of Puebla (1862). Festivities are held across the city on May 5. Every other car will be flying a huge Mexican flag.

June LA Pride is corporate, leaving the most fun for **West Hollywood Pride** (p174), the premier LGBTQ+ event. It draws vast crowds to the route and the bars and parties in the days before, during and after.

October The **West Hollywood Halloween Carnaval** attracts over half a million people to the world's largest Halloween street party. Outrageous, edgy and risqué outfits, dancing, a half-dozen stages of live music and lots of joyous fun.

Los Angeles Weather

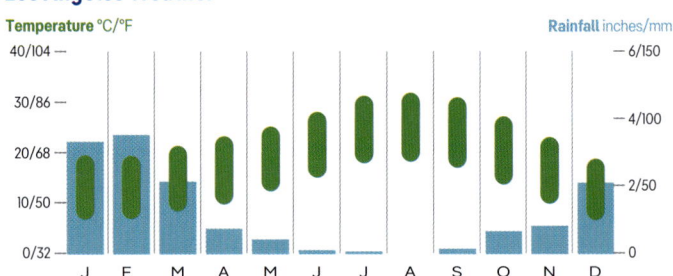

West Hollywood Pride (p174)

LA's Creative Spirit

March The **Academy Awards** are by far LA's biggest night and there's a palpable energy from Echo Park to Beverly Hills in the week beforehand. Fans can ogle the stars from bleachers outside the Dolby Theatre. Apply in November at *oscars.org* for one of around 700 lucky spots or watch the ceremony like a football game in a Hollywood bar.

April One of the world's largest literary gatherings, the **Festival of Books**, draws top authors, publishers and thousands of readers to the USC campus near Exposition Park over a weekend.

July The Hollywood Bowl bursts with color for the nighttime **July 4 Fireworks Spectacular**, LA's big fireworks show, which is accompanied by top music acts.

September Over a weekend, the **Watts Towers Day of the Drum Festival** uses the famed public folk-art sculpture (p92) as the centerpiece for gospel, jazz and R&B music.

ACCOMMODATIONS LOWDOWN

Book your accommodations in LA as early as possible. There's steady demand through the year, what with the many events, sports matches, conventions, weekend jaunts and year-round decent weather. Demand for more affordable lodging is even higher in summer, when families descend on the city.

✈ Getting There

LAX is the busiest airport; Burbank (BUR) also sees substantial traffic. Union Station receives Amtrak and regional trains.

From LAX to the City

By Train

LAX This rail service includes the new Metro K Line, which serves the LAX/Metro Transit Center station that opened in 2025. The line is part of the Metro Rail system, allowing easy access to destinations around town. Initially, the station was connected to LAX by shuttle bus. In 2026 the new Automated People Mover (APM), serving the terminals and the rental-car center, is scheduled to open, providing an all-rail link between LAX and the city.

By Bus

LAX FlyAway Buses travel non-stop to Downtown's Union Station (35 minutes to 1 hour) and Van Nuys (40 minutes to 1 hour). Trip times are subject to traffic conditions. For scheduled bus services, catch the free shuttle (labeled 'Lot South/City Bus Center') from the airport terminals to the LAX City Bus Center. From here, local buses serve LA County. For Santa Monica or Venice, change to the Santa Monica Big Blue Bus Line 3 or Rapid 3.

By Rideshare or Taxi

Rideshares and taxis are located at the LAX-it (pronounced 'LA Exit') lot, a three-minute walk east of Terminal 1. A free, frequent shuttle bus connects to all nine terminals.

Other Points of Entry

Hollywood Burbank Airport (BUR)

Convenient to Hollywood, Downtown LA and Pasadena, BUR has domestic and intrastate service from all major airlines, especially budget carriers. It is linked by Metro bus line 222 to the Universal City/Studio City stop on the Metro Rail B Line.

Union Station

Interstate trains on Amtrak, regional Metrolink trains and Metro Rail A, B and D Lines serve Downtown's historic Union Station.

John Wayne Airport (SNA)

Located close to Disneyland® in Santa Ana and best reached by car, it has domestic and intra-California service from all major airlines.

Getting Around

Getting around LA is both easier and harder than you think. It's harder because that famous traffic is worse than you thought; jams can even occur after midnight, and rush 'hour' runs long (7am to 10am and 3pm to 7pm). It's easier because billions have been spent on public transit and neighborhoods are walkable.

Rail

The Metro Rail network consists of two subway lines and four light-rail lines. Four lines converge in Downtown LA, where there are two subways tunnels, one for the B and D lines and one for the A and E lines. The most useful lines for visitors are:

A Line Light-rail line running Pasadena to Long Beach via Highland Park and Downtown.

B Line Subway linking Downtown's Union Station to North Hollywood via central Hollywood and Universal City.

D Line Subway between Downtown LA, Koreatown and Mid-City. The line's 2025 extension to Mid-City (p107) serves major attractions like LACMA. Further extensions will reach Beverly Hills and Westwood. They're scheduled to be finished in time for the 2028 Summer Olympics.

E Line Light-rail line linking East LA to Santa Monica via Downtown, Exposition Park and Culver City. It connects to the new K Line at the Expo/Crenshaw station.

K Line New light-rail line serving LAX via Inglewood. When open,

FROM LEFT: KAROLIS KAVOLELIS/SHUTTERSTOCK, KAROLIS KAVOLELIS/SHUTTERSTOCK

─── **ESSENTIAL APP** ───

TAP is the essential fare app for Metro and other Southern California transit systems such as Santa Monica Big Blue Bus.

the new Automated People Mover (APM) from the K Line's LAX/Metro Transit Center station will link the rental car center and nine terminals at the airport.

Most lines run from around 5am to around 12:30am. Frequency ranges from up to every five minutes during rush hour to every 10 to 20 minutes at other times.

Metrolink is the system of commuter rail lines serving the greater region based out of Union Station. The most useful line for visitors is the service to Anaheim for Disneyland® (p162).

Bus

Metro operates dozens of bus lines across the city in several flavors. Of interest to visitors:

Metro Local buses Painted orange; make frequent stops along major thoroughfares throughout the city.

Metro Rapid buses Painted red; stop less frequently and have sensors that keep traffic lights green when a bus approaches.

Santa Monica–based Big Blue Bus serves the Westside, including Santa Monica, Venice and Westwood. The Culver CityBus runs services throughout Culver City and the Westside.

DASH Bus

These small shuttle buses, run by the LA Department of Transportation (ladottransit.com), operate along 30 routes and serve local communities, but only until around 6:30pm to 7pm and with limited services on weekends. Many lines connect with other DASH routes as well as Metro Rail stations. Fares are only 50¢.

One useful route is Observatory/Los Feliz that runs from the Vermont/Sunset metro station (B Line) to Griffith Observatory.

Rideshare

Because of LA's size and traffic, getting around by cab or rideshare will cost you. However, rideshares, such as Uber and Lyft, are popular and are a handy way to bridge the 'last mile' from a Metro Rail station to your destination. Plus, when you compare the cost of parking etc, the fees look better.

Car

Having your own wheels is useful for exploring many parts of Southern California, although this means contending with some of the worst traffic in the country.

Parking is occasionally free; however, most places charge parking rates – some hefty. Street parking can be difficult to find. Valet parking at pricier restaurants is commonplace.

Bike

Metro operates a region-wide bikeshare system called **Metro Bike** (bikeshare.metro.net). Bikes can be brought onto Metro buses and trains. **BikeLA** has a great collection of online bike lane maps and more. *(la-bike.org/bike-maps)*

Public Transportation Essentials

Use TAP to Pay

To ride Metro trains and buses, use **TAP** *(taptogo.net)*, which works in several ways:

- Buy a physical card *($2)* from machines in rail stations. Top up at stations and on buses.
- Add a virtual TAP Card to your Apple wallet.
- Use the TAP app with any Apple or Android phone.

Note: the TAP system caps your spending at $5/18 per day/week. After that, all rides are free. Use TAP on other SoCal transit systems.

Trip Planning

To plan Metro trips, use *metro.net* or map apps.

TRAVEL COSTS

Bikeshare
$1.75 per 30 minutes

Daytime parking lot
$30 or more

Metro transfers
Free for two hours

TOP TIP

Fare evasion on Metro results in a $75 fine from ticket inspectors, although it can be more.

METRO TICKETS

Ticket	Cost
Single fare	$1.75
1-day fare cap	$5
7-day fare cap	$18

🎁 A Few Surprises

LA is a surprise everywhere you look. It's a city of clichés – some are true but many are not.

Find Your Favorite Location

There is no way to quantify the number of times LA has appeared in movies, TV shows and streaming series over the decades, both as itself and standing in for locations worldwide. Nearly every block in the city has been used by some production at some point.

You can go on tours led by others or you can go on your own self-guided jaunts pegged to your particular favorites. Each year, more and more people experience the thrill of being in the actual place where a favorite production created the magic that touched them. Top location tours are:

Movie Guys' L.A. Film Locations Tour (lafilmlocationstour.com) Customized to what you want to see.
Film Freak Tour (filmfreak.com/tours) Follows a set two-hour route from Hollywood that visits over 75 locations. See p160 for a round-up of the studio tours.

For researching your own tour:
Wikipedia Individual film entries often have production notes that are detailed and specific. Search on the name of the production and you'll likely find at least one of the many sites that track locations.
imbd.com Has plenty of information, but keep in mind that the info is crowd-sourced, so may not always be accurate.

Look Up to the Light

In the 1860s Los Angeles was installing gas streetlamps, and in the 1870s the switch was made to electric streetlights. As the city grew exponentially, so did the number of streetlights, and today there are over 220,000. But what few people notice is their variety.

LOS ANGELES FILM LOCATION NEIGHBORHOOD WALKS

See locations in **Hollywood** for Tarantino's *Once Upon a Time in Hollywood* and the shelter from 1953's *War of the Worlds*. (p43)

Stand in **Chinatown** where the climactic scene was shot in the namesake 1974 movie. (p59)

Start at a core location for the *Fast & Furious* films in **Echo Park**. (p75)

Gaze at the opening shot of *Gone with the Wind* in **Culver City**. (p111)

Streetlamp during sunset, Los Angeles

Across LA there are more than 400 different types of streetlight, and in a city that is often accused of being quick to throw out its past, many of these various types are more than 100 years old. The city's Bureau of Street Lighting maintains the original style of streetlights. In older neighborhoods, such as Echo Park, Boyle Heights or Highland Park, you'll see elegant designs with multiple glass globes and ornamental details, even when the bulbs are the latest energy-efficient LEDs. You can take virtual tours of LA's huge diversity – and artistry – of streetlights at the bureau's website *(lalights.lacity.org/about/museum .html)*. Keep looking up as you go around the city to see many how styles you can spot.

All the World's in LA

Like the United States itself, LA is built on immigration and it may be the most diverse city in the country. Pick a country or an ethnic group and you'll find it represented in LA. Just around Mid-City, you have Little Ethiopia (p115), restaurants with food from Tajikistan, blocks where Eastern European Jews live, and many, many more. Downtown, you can walk from Chinatown (p58) to Little Tokyo (p64) and on to Hispanic Boyle Heights (p68) in 20 minutes, and on and on. Look around as you move through the city and you'll travel the world.

Explore
Los Angeles

Hollywood 39
Downtown 53
Griffith Park, Los Feliz & Echo Park ... 71
Exposition Park & South LA 85
Pasadena & Highland Park 95
Koreatown, Miracle Mile & Mid-City ... 107
West Hollywood & Beverly Hills 121
Santa Monica 133
Venice & South Coast Beaches 145
Burbank & Universal City 155

Worth a Trip
Getty Center 130
Malibu 142
Disneyland® Resort 162

Los Angeles's Walking Tours
Strolling Old Hollywood 42
Walk Downtown's Ghosts 56
Walk Chinatown 58
Discovering Boyle Heights 68
Rambling Through Echo Park 74
Tour Expo Park on Foot 88
Walking Pasadena 98
Walk Culver City 110
Walk Beverly Hills 124
Stroll Santa Monica's Beach 136
Exploring Venice 148

Walt Disney Concert Hall, design by Frank Gehry (p62)
SHUTTERSV/SHUTTERSTOCK

See p50 for eating, drinking and shopping listings

Explore
Hollywood

Researched by
Ryan Ver Berkmoes

The Hollywood area might be past its heyday, but its history is rich in stories of Californian glamour, and the neighborhood is filled with iconic monuments that even the excessive souvenir shops and tour buses can't taint.

The Walk of Fame is part of the bread and butter of Hollywood, and millions of visitors come each year to stroll down the tawdry but bustling city blocks to see the terrazzo sidewalks with their celebrity stars. There are good restaurants and bars to be found here. And, yes, you can see a great movie – new or classic – in a golden-age movie palace.

Getting Around

 Metro
The B Line's three stations on Hollywood Blvd connect to Los Feliz, Downtown LA and Universal Studios.

 Bus
Metro Line 2 connects Sunset Blvd to West Hollywood and Westwood. Metro Line 4 connects Santa Monica Blvd to West Hollywood and Beverly Hills. Both bus lines reach Silver Lake, Echo Park and Downtown LA. The DASH Hollywood route runs a circuit around Hollywood.

 Car
Street parking is competitive and parking lots are expensive.

THE BEST

STUDIO TOUR Paramount
Pictures (p47)

MOVIE TREASURES
Hollywood Museum (p45)

GREAT ENTERTAINMENT
Hollywood Bowl (p47)

STORIED RESTAURANT
Musso &
Frank Grill (p50)

FAMOUS ICON
Hollywood Sign (p46)

Hollywood Boulevard during sunset (p44)
JOECHO-16/GETTY IMAGES

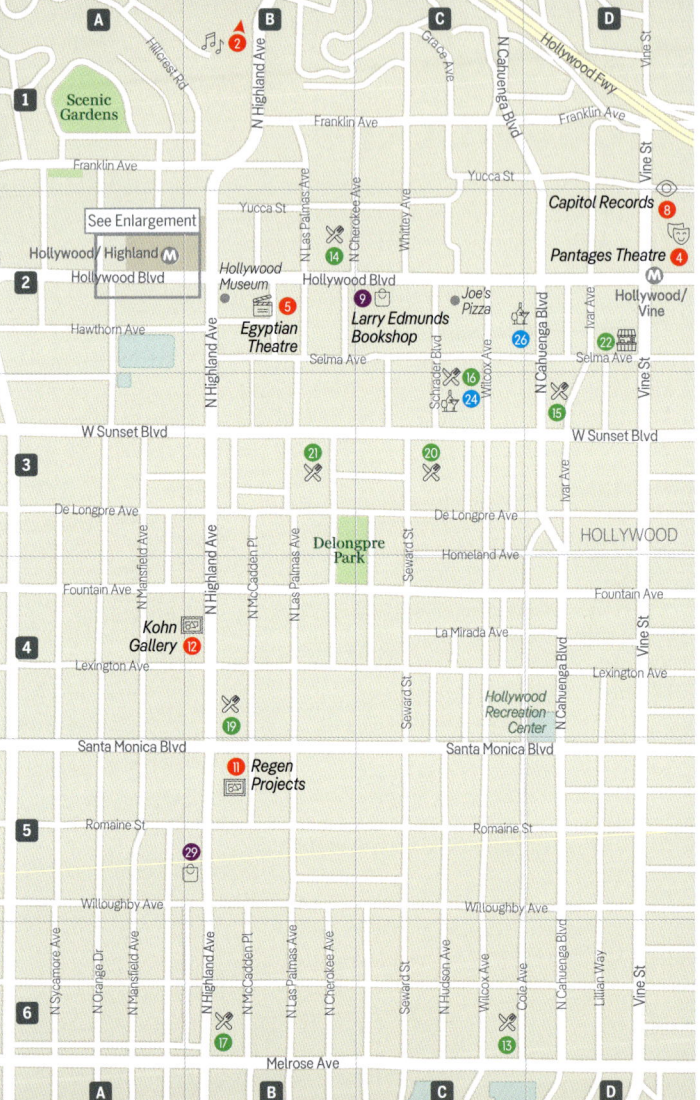

EXPLORE

HOLLYWOOD

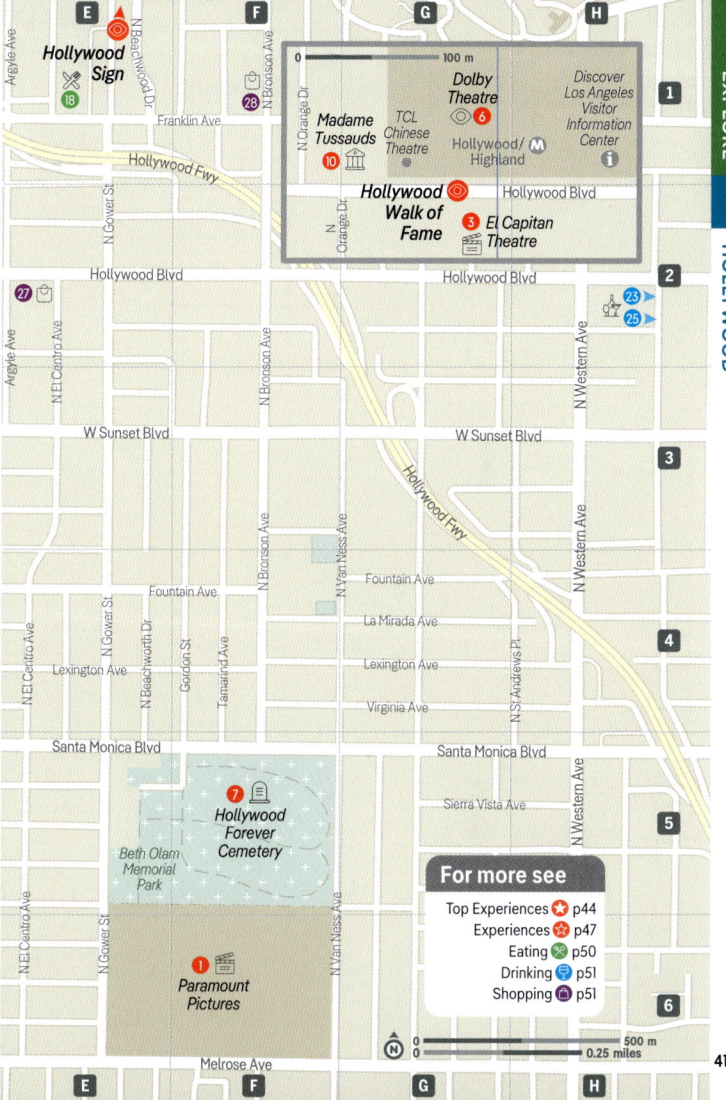

Argyle Ave

E

Hollywood
Sign

N Beachwood Dr

F

G

H

Dolby
Theatre
6

Discover
Los Angeles
Visitor
Information
Center

1

18

28

Franklin Ave

N Orange Dr

Madame
Tussauds
10

TCL
Chinese
Theatre

Hollywood/
Highland

Hollywood Fwy

Hollywood Blvd

N Gower St

N Orange Dr

Hollywood
Walk of
Fame

3 El Capitan
Theatre

27

Hollywood Blvd

Hollywood Blvd

2

Argyle Ave

N El Centro Ave

N Bronson Ave

N Western Ave

23
25

W Sunset Blvd

W Sunset Blvd

3

N Bronson Ave

N Van Ness Ave

Hollywood Fwy

N Western Ave

Fountain Ave

Fountain Ave

4

N El Centro Ave

N Gower St

N Beachworth Dr

Gordon St

Tamarind Ave

La Mirada Ave

Lexington Ave

N St Andrews Pl

Lexington Ave

Virginia Ave

Santa Monica Blvd

Santa Monica Blvd

N Western Ave

7

Sierra Vista Ave

Hollywood
Forever
Cemetery

Beth Olam
Memorial
Park

5

N El Centro Ave

N Gower St

N Van Ness Ave

For more see

Top Experiences ⭐ p44
Experiences 🌸 p47
Eating 🍽 p50
Drinking 🍷 p51
Shopping 🛍 p51

1

Paramount
Pictures

500 m
0.25 miles

6

Melrose Ave

41

E

F

G

H

WALKING TOUR

Strolling Old Hollywood

Hollywood Blvd was once the very heart of the movie industry. From the 1910s through the 1940s this strip and the surrounding blocks were where you found the stars, the producers, the talent scouts and the hangers-on. Today it lives on its past fame, but its storied history is everywhere and you'll feel it on this walk.

START	END	LENGTH
Hollywood Blvd/Vine St	Hollywood Heritage Museum	1.75 miles; 2 hours

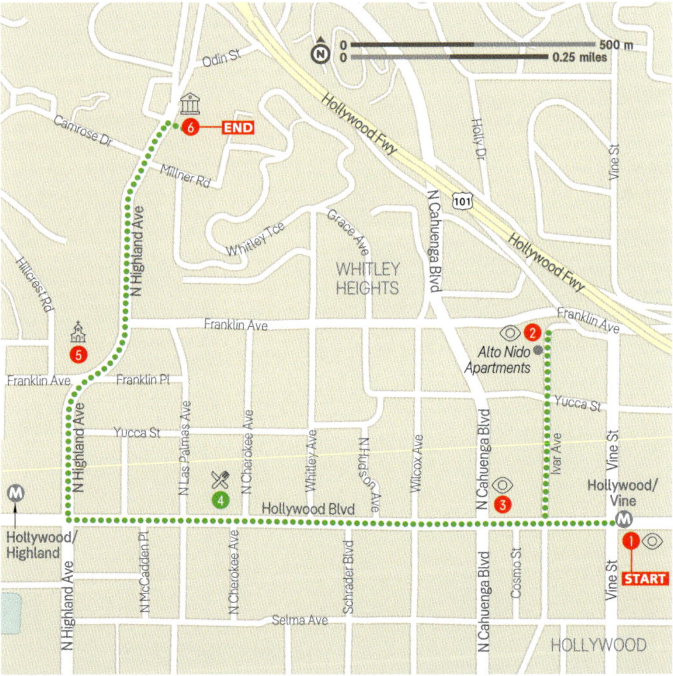

1 Infamous Corner

If you turned on the radio in the 1920s and '30s, the chances were you'd hear a broadcast 'brought to you from **Hollywood & Vine**'. At the intersection's southeastern corner is Hollywood's first high-rise office tower, the 12-story Taft Building (built in 1923). Former tenants include Charlie Chaplin and the Academy of Motion Picture Arts and Sciences.

2 The First Beverly Hills

For a taste of Old Hollywood, turn north up Ivar Ave to the narrow streets and beautiful Moorish, Renaissance and Italianate-style villas of Whitley Heights. This was the city's first 'Beverly Hills' and it was close to the silent-era movie studios. Highlights include the **Alto Nido Apartments** *(1851 N Ivar Ave)*, the location used for the initial home of the ill-fated Joe Gillis in *Sunset Boulevard.*

3 Marlowe's Office Building

Played by Humphrey Bogart in *The Big Sleep* (1946), noir detective Philip Marlowe appeared in books that author Raymond Chandler set in real LA locations. Back on Hollywood Blvd, the 1928 **Security Pacific Building** at the northeastern corner of Hollywood and Cahuenga Blvds is thought to be the location of Marlowe's dusty 6th-floor office where he waits for trouble to come through the door.

4 Tinseltown's Oldest Eats

More popular than ever, the **Musso & Frank Grill** (p50) has a history entwined with Hollywood. Chaplin came here to knock back vodka gimlets and Chandler penned scripts in the high-backed booths. It's a regular shooting location; recent appearances include *Once Upon a Time in Hollywood* and anything associated with writer Michael Connelly's detective Harry Bosch.

5 Soaring Church

Turn north at Highland Ave and head to the steeple of the **Hollywood Methodist Church**. Closely linked to the Hollywood community, the church was completed in 1930 and has long been a core part of the LGBTQ+ community. It was used as a location in *Back to the Future* and it was where panicked Angelenos sought refuge from aliens in *War of the Worlds* (1953).

6 Silent Hollywood

Hollywood's first feature-length film, Cecil B DeMille's *The Squaw Man,* was shot in this building in 1913–14, originally located at the corner of Selma and Vine Sts. DeMille went on to co-found Paramount and had the barn moved to the lot in the '20s. The building is now the fascinating **Hollywood Heritage Museum** *(hollywoodheritage.org; adult/child $14/free)*, which does a deep dive into pre-talkie history.

★ **TOP EXPERIENCE**

Hollywood Boulevard

Hollywood and fame – they're synonymous and they're symbiotic. Without fame, could Hollywood exist? Without Tinseltown, what would be our concept of fame? No matter the answer, a stroll along Hollywood Blvd makes it easy to dive deep into fame, with sidewalk stars, concrete handprints and four floors of celebrity treasures.

MAP P40 **G2**

PLANNING TIP

At least 30 stars are added to the Walk of Fame each year. Ceremonies often draw famous faces. Morning is best for exploring, as crowds are fewer and the boulevard is cleaner.

Scan this QR code for the schedule of Walk of Fame star ceremonies.

Follow the Stars

Hollywood Blvd is just tawdry enough that having an excuse to stare at the ground can be a good thing. The **Hollywood Walk of Fame** (walkoffame.com) gives you over 2800 reasons to keep your eyes down. Jennifer Lopez, Bob Hope, Marilyn Monroe and Aretha Franklin are among the luminaries of the big and small screens and the music industry that are sought out, worshipped, photographed and stepped on – or, in the case of many names, pondered over, since production staff and writers are also honored. They've been adding the brass and pink-terrazzo stars since 1960. Follow the galaxy along Hollywood Blvd between La Brea Ave and Gower St, and on Vine St between Yucca St and Sunset Blvd.

Famous Footprints

Compare your shoe size to George Clooney's or Tom Hanks' in the famous forecourt of **TCL Chinese Theatre** (tclchinesetheatres.com; forecourt free; pictured right). Complete with temple bells and stone heaven dogs from China, the exotic pagoda theater once known as Grauman's (first name Sid, who you'll see mentioned in the older imprints) has shown movies since 1927, when Cecil B DeMille's The King of Kings first flickered across the screen. It's not all feet: you can also see Betty Grable's legs,

GABRIELE MALTINTI/SHUTTERSTOCK

Whoopi Goldberg's braids, Daniel Radcliffe's wand and R2-D2's wheels. Inside, the cinema lives up to the promise outside. The theater is one of the world's few that can show 70mm film prints on an IMAX screen.

Hollywood Museum

Something of Hollywood's attic, the musty **Hollywood Museum** (*thehollywoodmuseum. com; adult/child $15/5*), a temple to the stars, is a mishmash of movie and TV costumes, props and memorabilia chaotically spread across four floors. The museum is housed inside the Max Factor Building, which launched in 1935 as a glamorous beauty salon for Hollywood's leading ladies. Track down the toupees worn by Frank Sinatra and John Wayne. A must-see is the 'Real to Reel' exhibit on LGBTQ+ issues in the industry.

QUICK BREAK
The dive bar **Frolic Room** (p51) is always ready for its close-up (eg *LA Confidential, Bosch*). For chewable fare, hit **Joe's Pizza** for authentic New York–style slices.

⭐ **TOP EXPERIENCE**

The Hollywood Sign

The 50ft-tall letters can be spotted easily from the corner of Hollywood Blvd and Highland Ave and myriad other spots in LA, including possibly on your flight in. 'HOLLYWOOD,' they proclaim in a robust, in-your-face typeface that doesn't fluff around. And you can get close.

MAP P40 **E1**

PLANNING TIP
Three hiking trails – Brush Canyon Trail, Mt Hollywood Trail and Cahuenga Peak Trail – lead to the sign, or you can go on a hiking tour (p126).

Scan this QR code for more details about the Hollywood sign.

Icon for a Century

LA's most visible landmark, the iconic **Hollywood Sign** is perched at the top of Mt Lee in the Hollywood Hills. The story goes that *Los Angeles Times* publisher and real estate developer Harry Chandler erected the sign in 1923 (back then it said 'Hollywoodland') as a way to advertise luxury homes in the hills.

What was only supposed to be there for 18 months became a permanent landmark that has come to symbolize a place, an industry and a mythology. The sign is now trademarked; don't even think of trying to use a similar typeface for your smoothie shop.

Sign of the Times

In 1932 a struggling young actress named Peggy Entwistle leapt her way into local lore from the letter 'H.' The last four letters were lopped off in the '40s as the sign started to crumble. In the late '70s Alice Cooper and Hugh Hefner joined forces with fans to save the famous symbol and raise the money needed for a full reconstruction (several letters were collapsing). In 2010, when the hills behind the sign became slated for a housing development, industry luminaries raised the $12.5 million it took to buy and preserve the land.

EXPERIENCES

Tour Hollywood's Last Great Studio

STUDIO VISIT

MAP: **1** P40 **F6**

The *Indiana Jones, Godfather* and *Ironman* series are among the blockbusters that originated at **Paramount Pictures**, the country's second-oldest movie studio (1914) and the only major one still in Hollywood proper.

Two-hour golf-cart tours *(paramountstudiotour.com; from $69)* of the studio complex are offered year-round, taking in the back lots and sound stages. Passionate, knowledgeable guides offer fascinating insights into the studio's history and the movie-making process in general. VIP tours include a meal, but are not worth the much higher fee. Fans of *Star Trek* will want to follow Leonard Nimoy Way to the sound stages where the original TV show was shot.

Hear Stars Under the Stars

OPEN-AIR MUSIC VENUE

MAP: **2** P40 **B1**

The Hollywood Hills stalwart **Hollywood Bowl** *(hollywoodbowl.com)* hosted its first concert in 1922. Headliners have ranged from Billie Holiday to the Beatles, and it's still the summer home of the LA Philharmonic. The amphitheater stands out for its unique silhouette, which is reminiscent of – you guessed it – a bowl, with concentric shell-like arches. This is a live-show summer haven for Angelenos, and although food and beverage prices can hit a high note (you can bring your own), the Hollywood Hills backdrop, the acoustics and the views make up for it all.

See a Show in a Palace

LAVISH CINEMAS

Hollywood's grand theaters are looking better than ever. Disney premieres blockbusters at the 1926 **El Capitan Theatre** (MAP: **3** P40 **G2**; *elcapitantheatre.com*); *Citizen Kane*

 HISTORY OF HOLLYWOOD

Few industries have symbolized Los Angeles more than moviemaking. Independent producers were attracted here, beginning in 1908, for Southern California's sunny climate, which allowed indoor scenes to be shot outdoors – essential given the unsophisticated photo technology of the day. And any location, from ocean to desert to alpine forest, could be realized nearby.

By the 1920s major studios had been established that controlled all aspects of production and distribution. Hollywood continued as a company town for decades, with dozens of major and minor players. This lasted until recently. However, AI, streaming and high costs are challenging Hollywood's hold like never before.

premiered here in 1941. The *Jimmy Kimmel Show* is produced here – book tickets at *1iota.com.*

Adorned with art deco chevrons, ziggurats, zigzags and octagons, the **Pantages Theatre** (MAP: ④ P40 D2; *broadwayinhollywood.com*) hosted the Academy Awards between 1949 and 1959, when Howard Hughes owned the place. It was the last of the great palaces built as the Great Depression closed in.

The **Egyptian Theatre** (MAP: ⑤ P40 B2; *egyptiantheatre.com*), the first of the grand movie palaces on Hollywood Blvd, premiered *Robin Hood* in 1922. The theater's lavish getup, complete with hieroglyphs and sphinx heads, dovetailed nicely with the craze a century ago for all things Egyptian. These days it's a shrine to serious cinema thanks to the nonprofit American Cinematheque and has enjoyed a lavish restoration thanks to Netflix, which is using it for premieres.

Tour the Home of the Oscars
FAMOUS THEATRE

MAP: ⑥ P40 G1

Since 2001 the Academy Awards have been handed out at the **Dolby Theatre** (*dolbytheatre.com; adult/child $25/free*), which has also hosted the *American Idol* finale, the ESPY Awards and the Daytime Emmy Awards. The venue is home to the annual PaleyFest, the country's premier TV festival, held in spring. Guided tours of the theater include viewing the auditorium, a VIP room and catching the shine of an Oscar statuette. Note: they also book big-name live acts here.

Stroll among Famous Graves
CELEBRITY CEMETERY

MAP: ⑦ P40 F5

Paradisiacal landscaping, vain-glorious tombstones and epic mausoleums (plus a view of Paramount Studios over the wall) at **Hollywood Forever Cemetery** (*hollywoodforever.com; free*) make an appropriate resting place for some of Hollywood's most iconic dearly departed. Residents include Rudolph Valentino, Cecil B DeMille, Mel Blanc (his tombstone reads, 'That's all folks'), Jayne Mansfield, Judy Garland, punk rockers Johnny and Dee Dee Ramone, *Golden Girls* star Estelle Getty, Burt Reynolds and David Lynch.

Check Out a Mid-Century Landmark
ICONIC BUILDING

MAP: ⑧ P40 D2

You'll have no trouble recognizing the 1956 **Capitol Records** tower, one of LA's great mid-century buildings. Designed by Welton Becket, it resembles a stack of records topped by a stylus blinking out 'Hollywood' in Morse code. Some of music's biggest stars have recorded hits in the building's basement studios, including Nat King Cole, Frank Sinatra, the Beatles, Katy Perry and Sam Smith. Outside on the sidewalk, Garth Brooks and John Lennon have their stars.

Hollywood's Literary Hub

MOVIE AND TV BOOKSTORE

MAP: **9** P40 **C2**

For decades the **Larry Edmunds Bookshop** *(larryedmunds.com)*, a cluttered old-school shop, has been the place to go for entertainment industry books, new and used. You can find out-of-print bios of long-dead celebs mixed with classic tomes on acting and scriptwriting techniques. Browse the bins of lobby cards for classic films and studio stills. There's a huge range of TV and movie scripts, and it hosts book signings with industry luminaries. Look on the walls for notable mementos, such as a check for a book purchase from Lucille Ball.

Ponder a Famous Likeness

WAX MUSEUM

MAP: **10** P40 **F1**

The better of Hollywood's two wax museums, **Madame Tussauds** *(madametussauds.com; from $35)* is the place to take selfies with motionless celebrities (such as Viola Davis, Salma Hayek and Harry Styles) and old-school icons (Charlie Chaplin, Marilyn Monroe and Clark Gable).

Go Gallery Hopping

GALLERIES

It's not all 'Lights, camera, action!' in Hollywood. Its list of assets also includes prolific commercial galleries specializing in modern and contemporary art. **Regen Projects** (MAP: **11** P40 **B5**) hosts bold, edgy shows across all mediums from photography, painting and video art

BEST FILMS ABOUT HOLLYWOOD

Sunset Boulevard (1950)

Billy Wilder at his best, plumbing the dark side of fame and Hollywood's delusions.

The Player (1992)

Robert Altman brings decades of experience on the front lines to this biting satire about the moral rot at the heart of studio execs.

La La Land (2016)

Timeless musical of plucky kids hoping to make it big in Hollywood.

The Artist (2011)

Won the Oscar for best picture for its story of the often-brutal late-1920s transition from silent pictures to talkies.

A Star is Born

Pick your version (1937, 1954, 1976 or 2018) of the classic drama about fame and tragedy.

to ambitious installations. It's well known for propelling the careers of some of Southern California's most successful and innovative artists, among them Matthew Barney, Andrea Zittel and Catherine Opie.

A short walk away, **Kohn Gallery** (MAP: **12** P40 **B4**) also offers museum-standard exhibitions, with both heavyweights (Li Hei Di and Barbara Kruger) and emerging talent (Sophia Narrett and Octavio Abúndez) on its books.

See p40 for map of locations

Best Places for...

$ Budget $$ Midrange $$$ Top End

Eating

Top Tables

Providence $$$
13 C6

Chef Michael Cimarusti's James Beard Award–winning, two-Michelin-star classic is known for turning superlative seafood into revelatory creations that never feel experimental for the sake of it. *6-9pm Tue-Sat*

Musso & Frank Grill $$
14 B2

History hangs in the air at Tinseltown's oldest eatery (since 1919). The menu favors American classics. Mixed drinks like the famous martinis come with sidecars on ice so your chaser is right at hand. Book ahead. *5-10pm Tue-Sun*

Grandmaster Recorders $$$
15 D3

Buzzing bistro with Italian flavors; the airy dining room was once home to the namesake recording studio. Today the hits are made in the kitchen. Rooftop bar and dining area with Hollywood vistas. *5-10pm Tue-Sat*

Mother Wolf $$$
16 C3

Superb Roman cuisine meets star power at this bustling restaurant. The 1930s art deco building recalls Hollywood's glamour days while today's celebrities provide the sparkle. Robust pastas, pizzas and superb desserts keep the crowds coming. *5-9:30pm*

Petit Trois $$$
17 B6

Owned by acclaimed TV chef Ludo Lefebvre *(Top Chef)*, Petit Trois has two long counters where fans squeeze in for smashing Gallic-inspired fare, from a wonderfully light Boursin-stuffed omelet to standout escargot. *noon-10pm*

Casual Favorites

Clark Street Diner $$
18 E1

Legendary diner (coffee shop in SoCal parlance) that's been in movies *(Swingers)* and served actors and writers nursing bottomless cups of coffee. Everything is flat-out boffo (oh, those blueberry pancakes!). *7am-9pm*

Trejo's Coffee & Donuts $
19 B4

Owned by Danny Trejo *(Heat, From Dusk Till Dawn)*, Trejo's is a standout in a town known for doughnuts. The goods reflect the owner's Mexican heritage. *7am-4pm*

Superba Food & Bread Hollywood $$
20 C3

This stylish version of a modern diner has an in-house bakery as well as breakfasts featuring alluring touches such as the candied pecans on the French toast. Also on offer are salads, sandwiches and a very good burger. *11am-10pm*

Luv2eat Thai Bistro $$
21 B3

Don't let the strip-mall location deter you. This haven for Thai food is

50

made all the more appealing by its location close to the Hollywood strip. Knockout choices include the Phuket-style crab curry. *11am-10pm*

Hollywood Farmers' Market
 22 **D2**

LA's largest farmers market is also one of its best. The Sunday-morning sprawl offers organic and specialty produce from local farmers, producers and artisans as well as tasty ready-to-eat bites and drinks. *8am-1pm Sun*

Drinking

Classy Pours

Harvard & Stone
23 **H2**

With daily rotating craft whiskey, bourbon and cocktail specials, Harvard & Stone lures partiers with its solid live bands, DJs and burlesque troops working their saucy magic. *9pm-2am*

Bar Lis
24 **C3**

All of Hollywood sweeps around you from this rooftop lounge on the 11th floor of the hip Thompson

Hollywood. Later, the tables are cleared and the dancing begins. *6pm-midnight*

Tabula Rasa Bar
25 **H2**

Thai Town's Tabula is everything one could want in a neighborhood wine bar: eclectic drops, unpretentious barkeeps, well-picked tunes and regular live gigs, including Sunday jazz. Offerings by the glass are short, sharp and engaging. *2pm-midnight*

Atmospheric Dives

Frolic Room
see **4** **D2**

The neon sign is worth a trip, but there's more here than colored lights. Anything goes at this true Hollywood dive that's served everyone from Judy Garland to Charles Bukowski. *11am-2am*

Burgundy Room
26 **C2**

Old Hollywood rocks on at the historic Burgundy Room, a grungy former speakeasy. You won't find seasonal cocktails here, just a timeless crowd of rockers knocking back cheap (for Hollywood) drinks to blaring blues and indie rock. *8pm-2am*

Shopping

Music, Books & Decor

Amoeba Music
27 **E2**

Flip through 500,000 new and used CDs, DVDs, videos and vinyl at this cult-status independent music hub, which also stocks books and comics. *11am-8pm*

Counterpoint
28 **F1**

Woodblock stacks are packed high with used fiction, while plywood bins are stuffed with vinyl soul, classical and jazz. Ask to see the hidden back rooms, home to the real gems. Staff recommendations show off diverse tastes. *noon-8pm*

JF Chen
29 **B5**

A go-to for professional curators, celebrities and their interior decorators, JF Chen offers two cluttered floors of museum-quality furniture and decorative arts from greats such as Poul Kjærholm, Ettore Sottsass and Charles and Ray Eames. *10am-5pm Mon-Fri*

See p66
for eating,
drinking and
shopping
listings

Explore
Downtown

Researched by
Ryan Ver Berkmoes

Ever surprising, Downtown LA is relatively small compared to other city centers in the US, and it's made up of smaller, diverse neighborhoods that all converge together.

Take Manhattan, add a splash of Mexico City and a dash of Tokyo, shake and pour. Your drink: Downtown LA. Rapidly evolving, DTLA (the preferred moniker) is the city's most intriguing patch, where cutting-edge architecture and killer modern-art museums contrast with a jumble of street life.

From the Arts District to Chinatown, from abject poverty to spectacular culture and from the LA of today to what feels like another place and time, DTLA is a heady, fascinating mix.

Getting Around

 Metro

Downtown has two subways: the B/D lines and the A/E lines. They all converge at the 7th St/Metro Center station. The A/B/D lines interchange with Metrolink commuter trains and Amtrak at historic Union Station.

 Bus

Metro buses connect Downtown to much of LA. DASH buses run five routes through Downtown.

THE BEST

ART MUSEUM
The Broad (p60)

MUSIC VENUE Walt Disney Concert Hall (p62)

BEST RIDE
Angels Flight (p63)

HISTORIC RESTAURANT
Philippe the Original (p66)

COLORFUL SHOPPING
Piñata District (p65)

View of Downtown LA during sunrise
IM_PHOTO/SHUTTERSTOCK

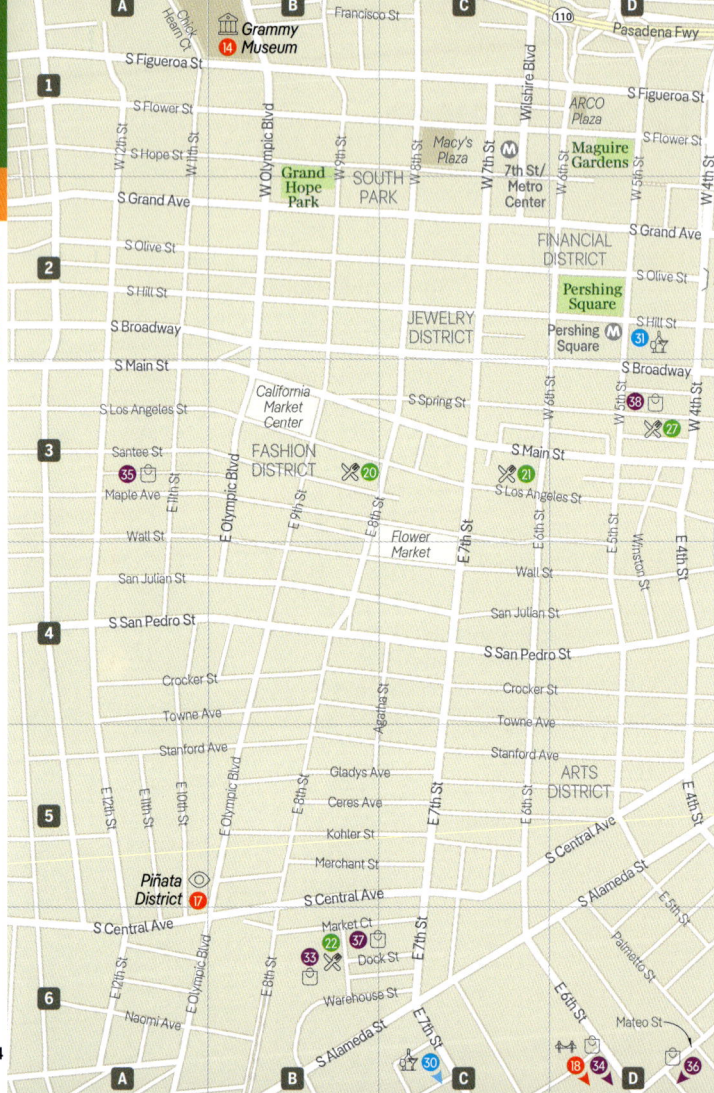

EXPLORE

DOWNTOWN

A   B   C   D

Francisco St

Pasadena Fwy
110

1

Chick Hearn Ct

🏛 *Grammy*
14 *Museum*

S Figueroa St

S Figueroa St

S Flower St

W 12th St
W 11th St

S Hope St
W 11th St

S Grand Ave

ARCO
Plaza

W Olympic Blvd

Grand
Hope
Park

SOUTH
PARK

Macy's
Plaza

Wilshire Blvd

W 7th St

M
7th St/
Metro
Center

W 6th St

S Flower St

S Figueroa St

Maguire
Gardens

2

S Olive St

S Hill St

S Broadway

S Main St

S Los Angeles St

FINANCIAL
DISTRICT

S Grand Ave

S Olive St

Pershing
Square

Pershing   M
Square   31

S Hill St

S Broadway

38

27

JEWELRY
DISTRICT

S Spring St

3

Santee St

35

Maple Ave

Wall St

San Julian St

California
Market
Center

FASHION
DISTRICT

E Olympic Blvd

E 9th St

E 8th St

20

S Main St

21

S Los Angeles St

W 6th St

E 6th St

E 5th St

W 4th St

S Grand Ave

S 4th St

Winston St

Flower
Market

Wall St

San Julian St

4

S San Pedro St

Crocker St

Towne Ave

Stanford Ave

E 12th St

E 8th St

E 9th St

E Olympic Blvd

E 8th St

Agatha St

E 7th St

S San Pedro St

Crocker St

Towne Ave

Stanford Ave

S 6th St

S Central Ave

ARTS
DISTRICT

S 4th St

5

Gladys Ave

Ceres Ave

Kohler St

Merchant St

Piñata
District   ◎
17

S Central Ave

S Central Ave

Market Ct

22   37

33   Dock St

S Alameda St

S 5th St

Painetto St

6

Naomi Ave

E Olympic Blvd

E 8th St

Warehouse St

S Alameda St

E 7th St

Mateo St

36

30

18   34

54

A   B   C   D

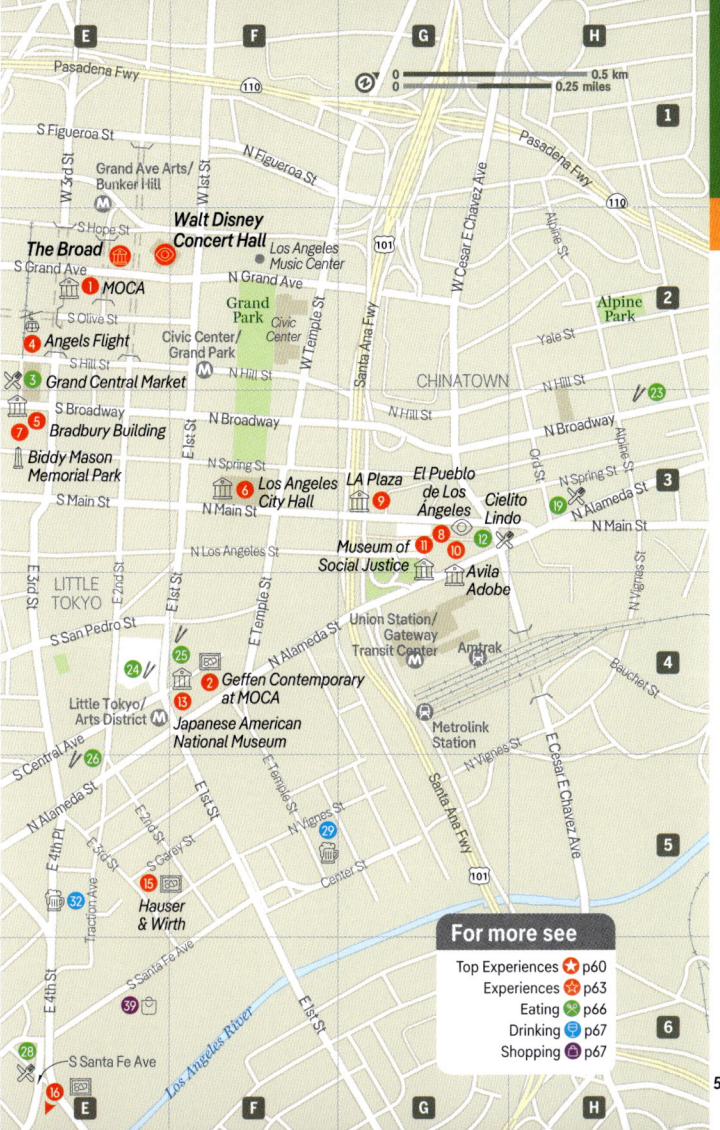

E   F   G   H

Pasadena Fwy
110

1

S Figueroa St
N Figueroa St

Grand Ave Arts/
Bunker Hill

W 3rd St
W 1st St

S Hope St

**Walt Disney
Concert Hall**
Los Angeles
Music Center

The Broad
S Grand Ave
N Grand Ave

1 MOCA
S Olive St

Grand
Park

Alpine
Park

2

4 Angels Flight
Civic Center/
Grand Park
Civic
Center

S Hill St
N Hill St

CHINATOWN

3 Grand Central Market
N Hill St

N Hill St

23

5 Bradbury Building
S Broadway
N Broadway
N Broadway

7

Biddy Mason
Memorial Park
N Spring St

S Main St

LA Plaza
El Pueblo
de Los
Ángeles

N Spring St
19

**6 Los Angeles
City Hall**
N Main St
9
Cielito
Lindo
N Main St

3

LITTLE
TOKYO

N Los Angeles St

Museum of
Social Justice
11
8
10

Avila
Adobe

E 3rd St
E 2nd St
E 1st St

S San Pedro St

Union Station/
Gateway
Transit Center
Amtrak

4

24
25

**2 Geffen Contemporary
at MOCA**

Little Tokyo/
Arts District

13

Metrolink
Station

S Central Ave
26

**Japanese American
National Museum**

N Alameda St
E Temple St
N Vignes St
E Cesar E Chavez Ave

E 2nd St
E 1st St

S 4th Pl
S 3rd St

29

5

Center St

32

15 Hauser
& Wirth
S Gerey St
Santa Ana Fwy
101

39

Traction Ave

S Santa Fe Ave

28

For more see
Top Experiences ⭐ p60
Experiences ⭐ p63
Eating 🍽 p66
Drinking 🍺 p67
Shopping 🛍 p67

S 4th St

16

S Santa Fe Ave
Los Angeles River

6

E   F   G   H

0   0.5 km
0   0.25 miles

110
N Figueroa St

101

W Cesar E Chavez Ave
Pasadena Fwy

Alpine St

Yale St

Old St

N Alameda St

N Main St

N Spring St

Santa Ana Fwy

Bauchet St

N Vignes St

E Cesar E Chavez Ave

WALKING TOUR

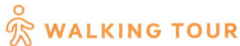

Walk Downtown's Ghosts

Downtown is the most historical and fascinating part of Los Angeles. Its streets are awash with the dreams of architects, designers and stars, translated into a cache of buildings both breathtaking and whimsical. Stroll through its multilayered streets to discover Downtown's gilded past and its unsettled future.

START	END	LENGTH
Eastern Columbia Building	Los Angeles Central Library	1 mile; 2 hours

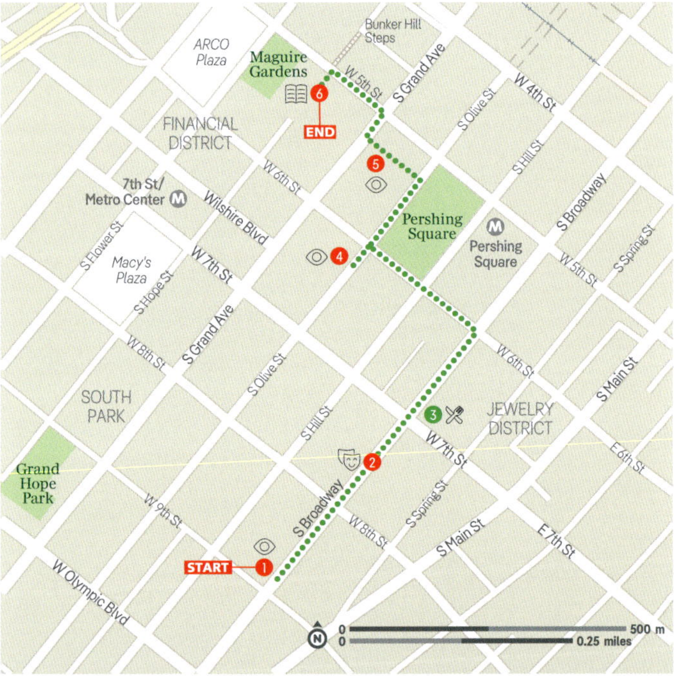

1 Eastern Columbia Building

Rising at the corner of 9th St and Broadway, the 13-story **Eastern Columbia Building** is a masterpiece of art moderne architecture, clad in highly glazed turquoise-and-gold terracotta tiles and featuring a gilded sunburst vestibule. Completed in 1930, its clock tower top is a landmark.

2 Broadway Theatre District

Spanning eight blocks of S Broadway from 11th St to 3rd St, the **Broadway Theatre District** once claimed the highest concentration of movie palaces in the world. The grand venues are in varying states of repair, but look for the marquees of the Belasco, Mayan and Orpheum and the restored Million Dollar Theatre, among others. At No 630, the **Palace Theatre** dates from 1911. Across Broadway, the lavish Los Angeles Theatre hosted the premiere of Charlie Chaplin's silent film *City Lights*.

3 Clifton's Republic

Opened in 1935, **Clifton's** was the flagship cafeteria of restaurant owner and social reformer Clifford Clifton. The son of missionaries, he founded organizations such as Meals for Millions and ran his cafeterias under his golden rule: diners should only pay what they think is fair and no one should ever be turned away hungry. In his spare time, he funded efforts to clean up LA's squalid and corrupt politics.

4 James Oviatt Building

From 1928 to 1967, Olive St's **James Oviatt Building** was home to fabled men's clothing store Alexander & Oviatt. Upon completion, the building's art deco lobby forecourt sparkled with 30-plus tons of glass by René Lalique, who also designed the mailboxes, directories and dashing doors of the time-warp elevators.

5 Millennium Biltmore Hotel

The Academy Awards were founded at a luncheon in 1927 at the **Biltmore Los Angeles**. The hotel's Historic Corridor features a fascinating photograph of the 1937 Oscars. Its screen credits are lengthy, including *Chinatown, Beverly Hills Cop* and even *Bachelor Party*. Pretty much any TV show that needed an opulent hotel interior dropped by to use the location as well, most recently *Hacks*.

6 Los Angeles Central Library

Designed by Bertram Grosvenor Goodhue, Downtown's **central library** opened in 1926. Head straight for the 2nd floor to admire its basilica-like rotunda, surrounded by the California-themed murals of Dean Cornwell in Technicolor. Look for nods to ancient Egypt throughout, such as the tiled mosaic pyramid crowning the central tower.

Walk Chinatown

Discover today's Chinatown, which is one of Downtown's most vibrant districts. This walking tour visits many of its lively mix of shops, restaurants and galleries, and it stops for treats. Along the way, you'll get a full dose of the neighborhood's history, going back to the era when official LA tried to make it go away.

START	END	LENGTH
Union Station	Chinese American Museum	2.75 miles; 2 hours

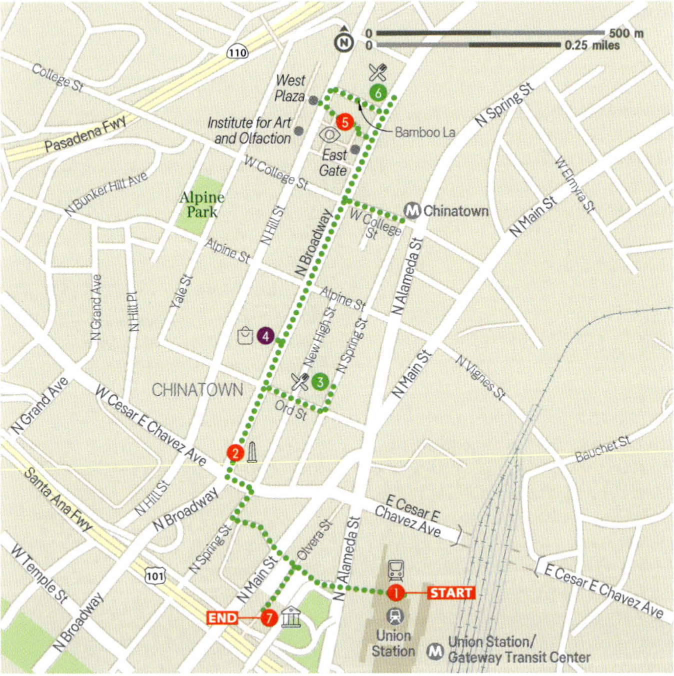

① Before Union Station

In the 1920s, LA's white leaders maneuvered to replace the city's Chinatown, which was deemed too close to the center of power, with what became the **Union Station** you see today. The Chinese population was moved several blocks north to today's Chinatown.

② Gateway to Chinatown

From the station, cross through El Pueblo de Los Ángeles to N Broadway, where there's the dragon-topped **Gateway Monument** (2001). Note the vendors, some with little more on offer than oranges they may have found on a tree. People sell all types of goods along Broadway every day.

③ Beloved Bakery

Cut around to N Spring St and **Long's Family Pastry**, where people line up for the $1.50 leek cakes. The final shot in *Chinatown*, with the line 'Forget it, Jake, it's Chinatown,' was filmed looking south in front of the bakery (with a lot of set dressing).

④ Mall of Delights

Return to Broadway and walk north. The small courtyard mall **Far East Plaza** is worth a pause for the Now Serving cookbook store, the vintage muumuu of your dreams at East/West Shop, the fanatical coffee preparation at Endorffeine and the exciting Filipino fare at Lasita Rotisserie & Natural Wine.

⑤ Neighborhood Center

Continue on Broadway until you see the East Gate. Enter Central Plaza (1938). Note the Bruce Lee statue (his martial arts studio was at 628 W College St). Cross Hill St to **West Plaza**, an appealing collection of small galleries. Follow your nose to the Institute for Art and Olfaction (*artandolfaction. com),* where you can take a class in creating scents or have one created for you.

⑥ Fresh Strawberry Cake

Back on Broadway, stop at **Phoenix Bakery** for a slice of its famous fresh strawberry cake. Across the street, Steep LA *(steepla.com)* holds regular tea ceremonies and classes. You might see baseball fans walking to nearby Dodgers Stadium. It was also used as a form of urban renewal (p80) by LA's power structure in the 1950s.

⑦ Old Chinatown's Museum

Cut over to the Chinatown Metro Rail stop for the one-stop ride to Union Station (or walk by retracing the same route, though the E-Train ride has great views), where the nearby **Chinese American Museum** *(camla.org; adult/child $3/2)* has full background on much of what you just saw. It's in the 1890 Garnier Building, one of the very few survivors of the demolished Chinatown.

⭐ **TOP EXPERIENCE**

The Broad

What do you do when you've got too much art to handle? Build a cutting-edge museum, fill it with your blockbuster acquisitions and share it with the city. That's exactly what Eli and Edythe Broad did, and their contemporary collection is considered one of the world's greatest.

MAP P54 **E2**

PLANNING TIP
Admission is free (except during special exhibitions), but reserve a timed ticket online. Once there, register to view *Infinity Mirrored Room*, as wait times can exceed an hour.

Scan this QR code for the Broad's excellent mobile museum guide.

A Stunning Building

Its name rhyming with 'road,' **The Broad** *(thebroad. org; free; pictured right)* is a must-visit for anyone with the slightest interest in postwar and contemporary artworks. It houses the collection of the Broads, local philanthropists and wealthy real-estate developers. With over 2000 pieces from artists such as Cindy Sherman, Jeff Koons, Andy Warhol, Roy Lichtenstein, Robert Rauschenberg, Keith Haring and Kara Walker, it's considered one of the most prominent holdings of 20th- and 21st-century artworks.

The striking building is an attraction in itself. Designed by NY–based firm Diller Scofidio + Renfro (designers of Manhattan's High Line) in collaboration with SF-based firm Gensler, it's shrouded in a lattice-like shell that lifts at the corners, allowing visitors to access the cavernous, undulating lobby.

Collections

Among the many blockbuster exhibits here is Yayoi Kusama's immersive *Infinity Mirrored Room*. When it's your turn to view the installation, you'll enter a room that's both an artwork and an entire world of light and color. With your reservation to see the work, you can tour the museum and you'll receive a text message when there's an opening for you to go in. Wait times are dynamic, as some people spend less time inside than you'd think.

Once you've eyed up the temporary exhibitions on the lobby floor, an escalator whisks you up through a narrow tunnel to the 35,000-sq-ft 3rd-floor gallery, where Jeff Koons charms visitors with his giant bunch of stainless-steel tulips. The surrounding galleries rotate works from The Broad's permanent collection. These include a second interactive installation by Yayoi Kusama, *Longing for Eternity*.

Visit Details

The museum docents are knowledgeable. The Broad has an excellent phone-friendly website, accessible with free wi-fi inside the museum. It has full descriptions of the art and the artists, gallery guides plus maps, and audio tours (bring headphones). A tour for kids is narrated by LaVar Burton.

TAKE A BREAK
For a choice of snacks and quick meals that will seem almost as extensive as the collection at The Broad, head three blocks southeast to the **Grand Central Market** (p63).

⭐ **TOP EXPERIENCE**

Walt Disney Concert Hall

An intoxicating blend of steel, music and psychedelic architecture, the eye-popping Disney, together with the neighboring museum The Broad, hit Downtown LA like twin meteors of 21st-century architectural ker-pow! And the buzz still resonates, much like the acoustics in this acclaimed concert hall.

MAP P54 **E2**

PLANNING TIP
The Walt Disney Concert Hall is such an amazing facility that it almost doesn't matter what you see here. Check for availability on the day of performances to experience it.

Scan this QR code to see what's on at the Music Center.

A Magnificent Concert Hall

The **Walt Disney Concert Hall** (*musiccenter.org*) is Downtown's eye candy. Its architect, Frank Gehry, designed a gravity-defying sculpture of heaving, billowing stainless steel. In contrast, the 2265-seat auditorium feels like a finely crafted cello, with walls of smooth Douglas fir and terraced seating wrapped around a central stage. You can visit, though the hall's best enjoyed at a concert by the **LA Philharmonic** (*laphil.org*) or other musical performances. The **Blue Ribbon Garden** honors Lillian Disney and her love of Royal Delft porcelain, which Gehry used to create a mosaic-like flower fountain.

LA's Music Center

The county-owned **Los Angeles Music Center** (*musiccenter.org*) complex is one of America's largest performing arts centers. Besides the Walt Disney Concert Hall, its multiple venues – the **Dorothy Chandler Pavilion**, **Mark Taper Forum** and **Ahmanson Theatre** – host resident companies including the **Center Theatre Group** (*centertheatregroup.org*), the **Los Angeles Master Chorale** (*lamasterchorale.org*) and the **Los Angeles Opera** (*laopera.org*).

Plazas with sculptures and a grand fountain link the venues. Before the advent of the Disney, the Chandler was LA's major performing arts venue and was the site of the Oscars for nearly 30 years.

EXPERIENCES

Thrill to MOCA   CONTEMPORARY ART

Adding to the superb collection of modern art in Bunker Hill is **MOCA** (*Museum of Contemporary Art;* MAP: **1** P54 **E2**; *moca.org; free*), whose 6000 works focus on pieces from the 1940s to the present. There's no shortage of luminaries, among them Mark Rothko, Agnes Martin, Elizabeth Murray, Willem de Kooning and David Hockney. Don't miss Jean-Michel Basquiat's neo-expressionist *Six Crimee*.

Check to see if there are temporary exhibitions at the **Geffen Contemporary at MOCA** (MAP: **2** P54 **F4**), down the hill in Little Tokyo.

Taste Grand Central Market   FOOD HALL

MAP: **3** P54 **E2**

Designed by prolific architect John Parkinson and once home to an office occupied by Frank Lloyd Wright, LA's beaux arts **Grand Central Market** (*grandcentralmarket.com; hours vary*) has been satisfying appetites since 1917 and today is DTLA's always-busy hub of food culture. Stalls and counters sell everything from fresh produce and nuts to sizzling Thai street food at **Sticky Rice**, hipster breakfasts at **Eggslut**, modern deli classics, artisanal pasta and specialty coffee.

Ride Angels Flight   FUNICULAR RAILWAY

MAP: **4** P54 **E2**

Built in 1901, the **Angels Flight** (*angelsflight.org; $1*) funicular originally shuttled commuters between Downtown and the long-gone Victorian abodes that graced Bunker Hill. The top end is fairly soulless and corporate, but the ride is an excursion into LA's past. It's starred in many productions, and fans of Michael Connelly's books and the *Bosch* TV series will get extra thrills.

Go for a Guided Walk   WALKING TOURS

Downtown LA's historical and architectural gems – from an art deco penthouse to a beaux arts ballroom and dazzling Union Station – are revealed on the nonprofit **Los Angeles Conservancy's walking tours** (*laconservancy.org; tours from $25*). The conservancy also offers an annual Last Remaining Seats season, screening classic films in gilded movie palaces.

Excellent self-guided driving and walking tours can be downloaded for free from the website.

Admire Two Iconic Buildings   FAMOUS ARCHITECTURE

The **Bradbury Building** (MAP: **5** P54 **E3**; 1893) is one of LA's heritage jewels. Behind its Romanesque-lite facade lies a whimsical galleried atrium that wouldn't look out of place in New Orleans. Inky filigree grillwork, rickety birdcage elevators and yellow-brick walls glisten golden in the afternoon light, which filters through the peaked glass roof. Such striking beauty hasn't been lost on Hollywood; it's been used in hundreds of productions, including *Blade Runner*.

Two blocks north is another instantly recognizable icon, **Los Angeles City Hall** (MAP: **6** P54 **F3**; 1928), the phallic-shaped star of *Dragnet, LA Confidential* and countless other films and TV shows. It hides a surprise on its 27th floor: a free **observation deck** (*9am-5pm Mon-Fri*) with incredible views of the city – when the smog allows.

Experience Biddy Mason Memorial Park   HISTORICAL PARK
MAP: **7** P54 **E3**
Stretching along a green and inviting alley behind the Bradbury Building and across from Grand Central Market, **Biddy Mason Memorial Park** details the incredible life of Biddy Mason. Born an enslaved person in Mississippi in 1818, Mason eventually moved to California, where she won a landmark court case in 1856 confirming her freedom. Working as a nurse, she began buying land – including this part of DTLA – and became a philanthropist to African Americans, the poor and the sick.

Stroll El Pueblo de Los Ángeles   HISTORIC NEIGHBORHOOD
Compact and popular, **El Pueblo de Los Ángeles** (MAP: **8** P54 **G3**; *elpueblo.lacity.org*) is the historic district where LA's first colonists settled in 1781. Wander through narrow **Olvera Street**'s vibrant and family-owned Mexican-themed stalls and check out the district's museums, the best of which is **LA Plaza** (MAP: **9** P54 **G3**; *lapca. org; free*), offering snapshots of the local Mexican American experience. The **Avila Adobe** (MAP: **10** P54 **G3**), built in 1818, is one of the region's oldest buildings. The heartfelt **Museum of Social Justice** (MAP: **11** P54 **G3**; *museumofsocialjustice.org; free*) examines LA's history through the filters of poverty, women's suffrage and civil rights. Have a taquito at the **Cielito Lindo** (MAP: **12** P54 **G3**; *9am-8pm*), the stand that claims their invention in 1923.

Explore Little Tokyo   HISTORIC NEIGHBORHOOD
To the north of Downtown lies **Little Tokyo**, a robust Japanese community that's been around since the early 1900s. Scores of shops and restaurants thrive across several blocks, and there's a traditional Buddhist temple.

At the center is the impressive **Japanese American National Museum** (MAP: **13** P54 **F4**; *janm.org*), which focuses on the evolution of Japanese American culture and gives moving insight into the mass incarceration of over 125,000 American citizens of Japanese descent in remote internment camps during WWII. Watch for temporary exhibitions while it undergoes renovations through late 2026.

Listen up at the Grammy Museum

MUSIC MUSEUM

MAP: **14** P54 **B1**

The highlight of the **LA Live** entertainment complex, the **Grammy Museum's** (*grammymuseum.org; adult/child $23/free*) interactive exhibits explore the evolution of popular music and the famous awards. Rotating exhibits might include iconic threads worn by Whitney Houston, Peggy Lee and Beyoncé, scribbled words from the hands of Count Basie and Taylor Swift, and instruments once played by music legends. Top names often perform.

Prowl the Arts District

ARTISTIC NEIGHBORHOOD

The **Arts District** is one of Downtown's most intriguing places. Blocks of old warehouses and gritty industrial areas have been cleaned up, and you never know what you'll find behind the big metal roller doors: gallery, designer shop or something more esoteric.

Among the swanky galleries, **Hauser & Wirth** (MAP: **15** P54 **E5**; *hauserwirth.com*) displays contemporary art and **Webber 939** (MAP: **16** P54 **E6**; *webberrepresents.com*)

LA'S STUNNING RIVER CROSSING
Opened in 2022, the striking **6th Street Viaduct** (MAP: **18** P54 **D6**) runs for over two-thirds of a mile, connecting Downtown's Arts District with the Boyle Heights neighborhood in East LA. Its overall design has won awards and continues to win new fans. Looping concrete arches in huge and varying sizes cross the Los Angeles River and two freeways at varying angles, while helical ramps accommodate cyclists. It's an ever-changing and vibrant look for what could have been a humdrum design. The previous viaduct was a beloved location used in myriad films and TV shows, including *Repo Man, Terminator 2: Judgment Day* and *Drive*.

has exhibits by famous names such as Yorgos Lanthimos.

Hit the Piñata District

NEIGHBORHOOD

MAP: **17** P54 **A5**

For the ultimate in single-use, colorful art, head to the busy **Piñata District**, where high-ceiling emporiums display legions of aliens, animals and other characters waiting for the big moment to spew forth candy when burst with a stick. Stores sell treats, and there are several huge and delicious open-air Mexican cafeterias with full bars.

See p54 for map of locations

EXPLORE

DOWNTOWN

Best Places for...

$** Budget   **$$** Midrange   **$$$ Top End

Eating

Casual Favorites

Philippe the Original $
19 H3

Famous old-fashioned joint renowned for French dip sandwich (go rogue: get pastrami instead of beef). Don't miss beets on the side. Always busy; sawdust on the floor. *6am-10pm*

Sonoratown $
20 B3

Superb northern Mexican street food, buttery tortillas with succulent, mesquite-grilled meats and excellent salsa. Sidewalk tables get busy at lunch; come early. *11am-10pm*

Cole's $$
21 C3

Dark, atmospheric, time-warped tavern claiming the invention (as does Philippe) of the French dip sandwich. The side dish of tater tots is a comfort-food classic; sublime pickles.

Great bar area and cocktails. *3pm-midnight*

Pizzeria Bianco $$
22 B6

Favorite pizza spot in Row DTLA has a shady terrace and some of Downtown's best thin-crust pies. Top ingredients, inventive specials, a good wine list and relaxed service make this a favored Arts District hangout. *11am-9pm*

Excellent Asian

Gigo's Cafe $
23 H3

Steamy, fragrant *pho* (Vietnamese noodle soup) is much sought after on this stretch of Broadway. Versions include classic thinly sliced rare beef *pho* as well as chicken and veggie versions. Bare-bones interior. *10am-7pm*

Shabu Shabu House $$
24 E4

A very humble Little Tokyo hot-pot joint with limited seating around a horseshoe bar illuminated with fluorescent lights. Always packed, and the tabletop pots are always steaming. *11am-10pm*

Marugame Monzo $$
25 F4

Join the queue at this hip udon emporium where noodles are made fresh and served hot or cold. Consider the creamy miso carbonara udon, a cult-status, East-meets-West creation. *11:30am-9pm*

Sushi Gen $$
26 E5

Grab a lunch seat in Little Tokyo; chefs carve slabs of the freshest fish. Dinner is less frenetic: get an actual table to enjoy the great-value sashimi. *11am-2pm & 5-8:30pm Tue-Sat*

Top Tables

Orsa & Winston $$$
27 D3

Progressive, well-executed Italian-Asian fusion flavors the five-course tasting menus here. Dinner's an adventure, with seasonal ingredients prepared in new and surprising ways. *5-10pm Tue-Sat*

Bavel $$$
28 E6

Sleek, loud and showered in cascading vines, with phenomenal, modern takes on Middle Eastern classics and pastry-driven desserts. Superb cocktails seal the deal. *5-11pm*

Drinking

Bars & Watering Holes

Boomtown Brewery
 29 F5

Great brews served inside and out, Downtown, with a steady parade of food trucks turning up. Pool tables, great party vibe and local art. *4-10pm*

Everson Royce Bar
30 C6

Arts District bar that puts the happy in happy hour. Suitably artful cocktails, best enjoyed in the shady backyard after a day wandering galleries and boutiques. *4-10pm*

Perch
31 D2

Two elevators get you to this French rooftop bar-restaurant in the Renaissance Revival Pershing Square Building. Gatsby vibe, with Manhattan-esque views. *4pm-1am*

Arts District Brewing Co
32 E5

Warehouse brewery in the Arts District, with brewing vats behind the bar, vintage Skee-Ball tables and a Charles Bukowski quote glowing in blue neon. Offers a big range of beers. Good food. *noon-midnight*

Shopping

Fashion Centers

Row DTLA
33 B6

This big center has transformed a sprawling industrial site into a curated garden of specialty retail and dining delights across several big warehouses next to a produce market. *hours vary*

Dover Street Market
34 D6

A sprawling, off-the-radar warehouse in which bleeding-edge fashion and art collide to spectacular effect and TikTok kids shoot videos out front. Idle browsing is rewarded with constant surprises. *hours vary*

Santee Alley
35 A3

Scores of alley vendors with bargains in clothing, bling and eyewear. Over 150 vendors between Santee St and Maple Ave, from Olympic Blvd to 12th St. *hours vary*

Designer Items

Good Liver
36 D6

Carefully curated Arts District space selling beautiful artisan objects uncommon in other design stores. Each object is displayed with a thoughtful note about the story and craftsmanship behind the object. *11am-7pm Tue-Sun*

Omami Mini
37 B6

Row DTLA has fashion-forward boutiques that set trends. This is clothing for the well-dressed under-12. Lots of comfy cotton wear. *11am-5pm*

Bookstores

Last Bookstore
38 D3

LA's largest new-and-used bookstore spills across two sprawling levels of an old bank building. Rare tomes, terrific vinyl collection, good prices and staff recs. Display of books banned in parts of the US. *11am-8pm*

Hennessey + Ingalls
39 E6

Light-filled Arts District new-and-used bookstore focuses on design, from architecture, interiors and landscaping to graphics, fashion and photography. Good set-design section. *11am-7pm*

🚶 **WALKING TOUR**

Discovering Boyle Heights

See where LA's mariachi bands wait for gigs, then wander a neighborhood built on immigration and full of unique businesses. In a city of melting pots, Boyle Heights has been the center of the flame from the start. Long Hispanic, it bears traces of Eastern European Jews, African Americans, Japanese and other groups.

START	END	LENGTH
Mariachi Plaza Metro stop	Hollenbeck Park	1.6 miles; 2 hours

1 A Tuneful Square

Start at **Mariachi Plaza**, which is also a Metro Rail stop (the colored-glass main canopy is evocative of a Mexican folk dancer's fan). Professional mariachi musicians dressed in their traditional *charro* suits have been descending on the old-school *zócalo* (public square) since the 1930s, waiting for work in the shade of the gazebo. The bands are available for last-minute gigs, not just a song or two.

2 Lively 1st Street

Heading east, **1st Street** is alive with businesses. **Un Solo Sol** serves vegan Latin American dishes; the banana-date shakes are a rich treat. A couple of doors down, **La Casa del Mariachi** supplies the mariachis with embroidered suits. Across 1st St, **Espacio 1839** is a community arts space. Back across the street, the **Women's March Store** supports the group's political activities with merch.

3 Bustling Cesar Chavez Avenue

Cross under I-5 and walk up the 1920s residential Cummings St to **Cesar Chavez Avenue** and turn east. **Other Books** is packed with comics and zines. Following are blocks lined with mom-and-pop retail. Among the notables is **Las Fotos Project** (*lasfotosproject.org*), which teaches teenage women of color about the power of photography. See if it has a show on.

4 1922 Synagogue

Turn south on N Breed St to step back to a previous era at the **Breed Street Shul Project**, which is restoring the 1922 Byzantine Revival synagogue. From 1910 to 1950 Boyle Heights was home mostly to immigrants from Eastern Europe and it had the largest Jewish population west of Chicago. The building was damaged in a 1987 earthquake.

5 Burrito Pioneer

Back at 1st St, turn west and go two blocks. Tiny **Al & Bea's Mexican Food** is so old (1966) it was a burrito pioneer in LA. The tiny storefront is grafted onto the Victorian home to the rear – this was once typical of how family-run businesses were set up. Close by, **Botanica Olokun** stocks spiritual candles.

6 Knocked-Around Park

At St Louis St, turn south three blocks. **Hollenbeck Park** in the 1890s was a palatial gem. As the neighborhood shifted to immigrants, its status changed and Victorian gingerbread details like bridges and ornamental gardens were removed. After WWII, Boyle Heights was seen as fertile ground for freeways, and five were rammed through, destroying over 11,000 homes. Today, I-5 support pillars rise from the lake.

See p81
for eating,
drinking and
shopping
listings

Explore
Griffith Park, Los Feliz & Echo Park

Researched by
Ryan Ver Berkmoes

From the natural heights and artificial diversions of Griffith Park, LA trendy neighborhoods of Los Feliz, Silver Lake and Echo Park offer hipsterism, laid-back vibes and urban charms unlike anywhere else in the sprawling city.

Griffith Park is a refreshing escape from the hustle and bustle, with its rugged, trail-laced hills and iconic Griffith Observatory offering some of LA's best views. South is walkable Los Feliz with its shops and nightlife along Vermont Ave and Sunset Blvd. The latter flows into ever-trendy Silver Lake and its diversity of food and people. Echo Park nears Downtown and mixes urban beauty with funky charm.

Getting Around

Bus
Metro Lines 2 and 4 run along Sunset Blvd; Line 2 buses then head south on Alvarado St. Line 2 reaches Hollywood, West Hollywood and Westwood. Line 4 reaches Downtown, Hollywood, West Hollywood and Beverly Hills. All reach Echo Park.

Metro
The B Line connects to Hollywood, Universal Studios and Downtown LA. Vermont/Santa Monica station lies 0.7 miles west of Sunset Junction in Silver Lake. Alight at Vermont/Sunset station for Los Feliz.

THE BEST

OUTDOOR LA
Griffith Park (p76)

VIEWS NEAR & FAR Griffith Observatory (p78)

BALL GAME Los Angeles Dodgers (p79)

MUSIC BY NIGHT
Dresden Lounge (p80)

CLASSIC MOVIES
Vista Theater (p79)

Griffith Observatory (p78)
SEAN PAVONE/SHUTTERSTOCK

For more see

✪	Top Experiences p76
✪	Experiences p79
✗	Eating p81
🍷	Drinking p82
🛍	Shopping p82

0.5 miles
1 km

Glendale Blvd

Brunswick Ave

Golden State Fwy

Riverside Dr

Los Angeles River

Riverside Dr

Rowena Ave

Rowena Reservoir

Hyperion Ave

Snow White Cottages

Los Feliz Blvd

Golden State Fwy

Crystal Springs Dr

Griffith Park & Southern Railroad

St George St

Autry Museum of the American West

Griffith Park

Griffith Park

Commonwealth Ave

Franklin Ave

Hillhurst Ave

Vista del Valle Dr

Roosevelt Municipal Golf Course

N Vermont Ave

N Vermont Ave

Los Feliz Blvd

N Vermont Canyon Rd

Mt Hollywood (1625ft)

Greek Theatre

Griffith Observatory

Observatory Rd

Western Canyon Dr

Fern Dell Dr

Finley Ave

Franklin Ave

N Vermont Ave

Brush Canyon Trail

Mt Hollywood Dr

Brush Canyon

Canyon Dr

Bronson Canyon

Bronson Caves

Trails

Franklin Ave

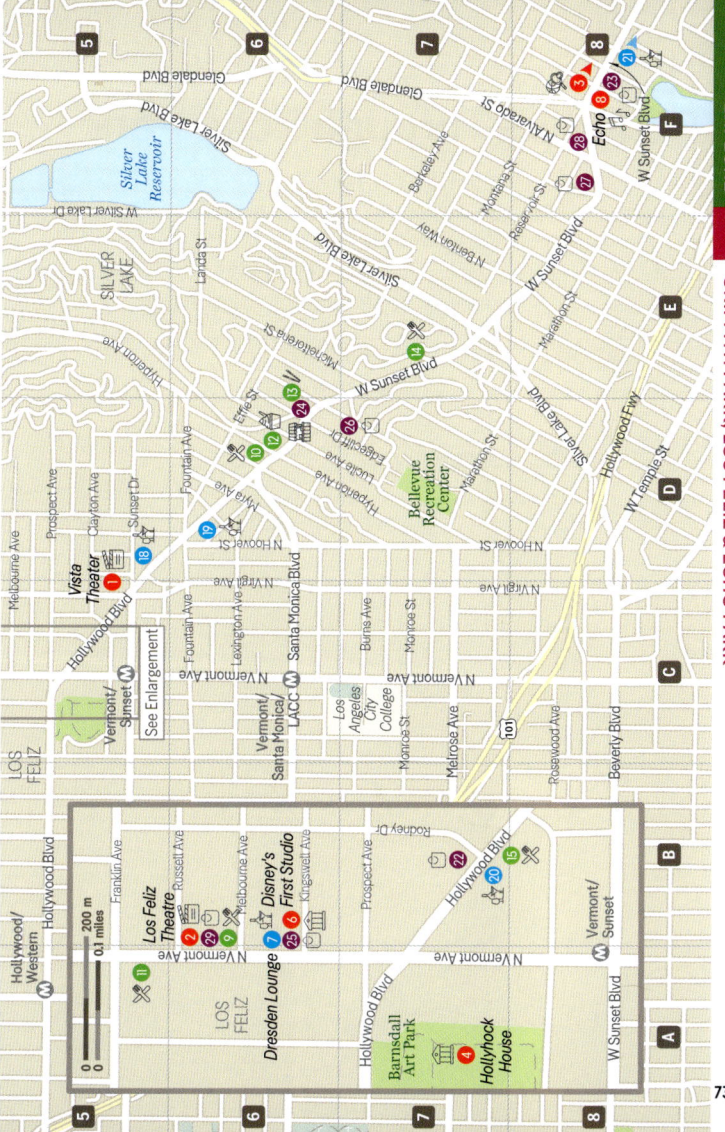

WALKING TOUR

Rambling Through Echo Park

Plunge into a classic LA mix of urban art, music, vintage shops and hipster culture in the multiethnic neighborhoods of Echo Park. The landmark lake and fountain are looking spiffy after a revamp, as are the Victorians up on Carroll Ave. Happily, the decades of the neighborhood's fabric remain amid the constant change.

START	END	LENGTH
Bob's Market	Angels Point	3.25 miles; 3 hours

❶ A Famous Market

Begin at **Bob's Market** (1913), aka Toretto's Market & Deli, owned by Vin Diesel's character in the *Fast & Furious* franchise. Look for the shelf of merch and the constant pack of fans out front snapping selfies. Walk up Bellevue Ave, turning right on Edgeware Rd into Angelino Heights, which was established in the mid-1880s as one of LA's first suburbs.

❷ Victorian Homes

The **1300 Block of Carroll Avenue** is home to the largest concentration of Victorian-era homes in the city. A few house numbers of note: 1300 is the grandest on the block, 1316 captures the look of the 1880s with its old-style drapes, 1329 was Halliwell Manor in the TV series *Charmed,* 1330 has Asian details and 1337 is the oldest house on the block (1872).

❸ Paddle the Lake

Walk down via Bellevue Ave to **Echo Park Lake**, a former reservoir. It's best known as the setting for Jake Gittes' surreptitious rowboating shenanigans in his quest for blackmail photos in *Chinatown.* Enjoy the keyhole vistas of the Downtown skyline, then find the boathouse amid the lush gardens and rent a swan-shaped pedal boat. After, stroll the perimeter.

❹ Sunset Boulevard's Shops

Go one block north on Logan St to Sunset Blvd. The cool retail includes the literature-rich **Stories** (p83), which has interesting LA-themed books. Close by, the indescribable **Time Travel Mart** (p82) has unusual goods related to concepts of time. You won't regret a minute you spend inside. Across the street, the **El Ruso** food truck serves famous tacos. It featured on Netflix' *Taco Chronicles.*

❺ Big Elysian Park

Walk north up Portia St and use your map app to wander through leafy **Elysian Park**. The verdant 600 acres here are low profile but ideal for a picnic procured at one of the shops back along Sunset Blvd. Note that Stadium Way, the main north–south road, was once more evocatively known as the Avenue of the Palms.

❻ Incredible View

Follow N Boyleston St and then walk up the paths near the entrance to Dodger Stadium parking. Look for the towering public art by LA artist Peter Shire. In its shadow you'll find **Angels Point**, one of the city's hidden gems. Here there are relatively unknown sweeping views of LA, taking in Dodger Stadium, Downtown and Hollywood. And there's never a crowd.

Griffith Park

Spanning the Hollywood Hills between the San Fernando Valley and central LA, **Griffith Park** is home to the Griffith Observatory and Autry Museum. LA's communal backyard covers more than 4300 acres of land, with over 50 miles of hiking trails across unspoiled chaparral.

MAP P72 **D1**

PLANNING TIP
See what's on at the Greek Theatre (*lagreektheatre. com*), the 5900-capacity outdoor amphitheater tucked into a woodsy Griffith Park hillside. It's a more intimate version of the Hollywood Bowl.

Scan this QR code for details on the park and its many attractions and activities.

Pick a Train Ride

Families can spend a day riding miniature trains in Griffith Park; each of the three options has distinct appeal.

Closest to Los Feliz, the **Griffith Park & Southern Railroad** (*griffithparktrainrides.com; adult/child $4/3*) has ferried generations of parents and kids on pint-sized trains around a 1-mile loop past an old Western town since 1948. Everyone loves the soft-serve ice-cream stand. **Travel Town** (*travel town.org; free*) is the park's railroad museum with a collection of moth-eaten railcars and locomotives that once rolled along the tracks in the Western US. There's a **miniature train** you can ride that meanders around the full-size collection. A huge model-train set-up is an ideal rainy-day idyll. Right next door, **Los Angeles Live Steamers** (*lalsrm. org; $4*) is a group of hobbyists who give rides most Sundays on their own miniature loop of track.

Hike to a Famous Cave

Griffith Park is LA's great hub of hiking, accessible from all directions and offering all types of experiences. A good start is the family-friendly short (0.7 miles one way) jaunt up **Bronson Canyon** off Canyon Dr to **Bronson Caves**. The latter are legit stars: among many appearances, they were the Bat Cave in the old *Batman* TV series and were the climactic lo-

TREKANDSHOOT/SHUTTERSTOCK

cation in *Invasion of the Body Snatchers* (1956). From here, various challenging trails (pictured above) lead to sights like the **Hollywood Sign** (p46).

Learn about the American West

Established by Gene Autry, known as the 'singing cowboy' and a successful television mogul in the 1950s, the expansive, underrated **Autry Museum of the American West** *(theautry.org; adult/child $19/8)* offers contemporary perspectives on the history and people of the American West, linked to today's culture. Exhibitions span Native American traditions, 19th-century cattle drives, daily frontier life (look for the beautifully carved saloon bar) and artifacts from Hollywood Westerns. More topical sections explore the use of the West for prisons, Indian treaties that were never ratified and African American cowboys.

QUICK BREAK
Follow Western Canyon Rd to where it becomes Fern Dell Dr at one of the southern entrances to the park for freshly baked goods and sandwiches at the outdoor cafe Trails.

★ **TOP EXPERIENCE**

Griffith Observatory

LA's landmark 1935 **observatory** opens a window onto the universe from its perch on the southern slopes of Mt Hollywood. It also offers prime views of much closer attractions, from much of Los Angeles to the nearby Hollywood Sign. It's also a famous film location.

MAP P72 **B3**

PLANNING TIP
Visit the observatory on a clear day to make the most of the spectacular views of the entire LA Basin, surrounding mountains and Pacific Ocean.

Scan this QR code for full opening hours and to buy planetarium tickets.

Samuel Oschin Planetarium

The observatory's **planetarium** is one of the world's finest, with a state-of-the-art Zeiss star projector, a digital projection system and a high-tech aluminum dome that transforms into a giant screen.

Finding parking can be akin to finding life on another planet. It's best to arrive on a weekday before noon. Otherwise, you may park so far away that you might as well hike up the hillside from Los Feliz (it's a great trail). Or, take the DASH Observatory/Los Feliz shuttle from the Vermont/Sunset metro station.

Leonard Nimoy Event Horizon Theater

A 24-minute documentary screened in the **Leonard Nimoy theater** is narrated by the late *Star Trek* actor himself. The *Edge of Space* shows objects that came to Earth through space or via space probe.

Telescopes, Views & Jimmy Dean

The rooftop viewing platform offers boffo views of LA and the Hollywood Hills. Visitors can peer into the telescope on the east side of the roof; after dark, staff put additional telescopes onto the front lawn.

It's made cameos in numerous movies and TV shows, but the observatory is best associated with *Rebel Without a Cause,* a fact commemorated with a **bust of James Dean** on the west side of the lawn.

EXPERIENCES

Watch Great Movies
CLASSIC CINEMAS

Dating to 1923, the single-screen **Vista Theater** (MAP: ❶ P72 **C5**; *vistatheaterhollywood.com*) has received a 100th-anniversary revamp of its wonderfully kitsch 'ancient Egyptian' interior from its owner Quentin Tarantino. He programs an eclectic lineup of mostly classic films (many from his own collection), projected in 35mm as opposed to digital. The director also runs the adjoining **Pam's Coffy** *(8am-7pm)*, a cafe dedicated to actor Pam Grier.

Just up the road, the century-old **Los Feliz Theatre** (MAP: ❷ P72 **B6**; *vintagecinemas. com*) is a gem of a neighborhood cinema. It screens first-run movies and a good mix of classics and arthouse films.

Cheer the LA Dodgers
BASEBALL

MAP: ❸ P72 **F8**

Few teams can match the **Los Angeles Dodgers** *(mlb.com/ dodgers)* for history (Jackie Robinson, Sandy Koufax, Fernando Valenzuela and sportscaster Vin Scully), success and fan loyalty, especially after they won an eighth World Series title in 2024. You see Dodger blue everywhere, and current sensation Shohei Ohtani is LA's most popular person.

Mid-century **Dodger Stadium**, between Echo Park and China-town (built on what was once the vibrant Mexican American neighborhood of Chavez Ravine; see p80), is considered one of baseball's most scenic, framed by views of palm trees and the San Gabriel Mountains. Buy tickets well ahead; games sell out.

See UNESCO-Recognized Hollyhock House
HISTORIC BUILDING

MAP: ❹ P72 **A7**

In 1919, oil heir Aline Barnsdall commissioned Frank Lloyd Wright to design **Hollyhock House** *(hollyhockhouse.org; adult/ child $12/free)*. With its central courtyard, porches and pergolas, the home is seen as a transitory moment in the architect's style, which evolved into a more open-plan, indoor-outdoor vision that would help define modern Southern Californian living.

It was declared LA's only UNESCO World Heritage Site in 2019, and the building's aesthetic evokes Mayan temple architecture, popular at the time it was built. The surrounding **Barnsdall Art Park** has grand views.

Ponder the Snow White Cottages
HISTORIC BUILDINGS

LA had a love for storybook houses between the 1920s and '30s, and prime examples are the **Snow White Cottages** (MAP: ❺ P72 **E4**). Built by developer Ben Sherwood in 1931, the eight white houses have thatched roofs, sweet window boxes and chimneys. They're said to be the inspiration for *Snow White and the Seven Dwarfs* (1937) and were built in ersatz Tudor style. The cottages stand just around the corner from the 1926–40 site of Walt Disney's studios (now a supermarket) on Hyperion Ave.

Disney's first studio (MAP: ⑥ P72 **B6**), now a copy shop, can be seen at 4647 Kingswell Ave in Los Feliz. Mickey's face peers out the window. Employees claim they sense the ghost of Walt every day.

Hear Crooners at the Dresden
MUSIC LOUNGE

MAP: ⑦ P72 **B6**

This institution has been serving LA crowds since 1954, and you may have seen it in the film *Swingers* (1996), where the line 'You're so money' was made famous. The **Dresden Lounge**

(*thedresden.com; 5pm–midnight*) is an old-school, retro-style bar and restaurant with dimly lit rooms, arched walkways and red-wine-colored booths. It was once known for singers Marty and Elayne, and their tuneful traditions are carried on nightly by an array of talented crooners (no cover!). This is definitely the place to savor a traditional cocktail – try the sidecar.

Rock to Bands at the Echo
MUSIC VENUE

MAP: ⑧ P72 **F8**

The **Echo** (*theecho.com*) is a crowded dive bar with a stage and a back patio. It's known for punk rock, but other styles here include indie, electronica, dub reggae, dream and power pop. Monday nights are the domain of up-and-coming house bands. The **Echoplex** downstairs is even more alt.

 THE FATE OF CHAVEZ RAVINE

Chavez Ravine, the piece of land where Dodger Stadium sits, has the sort of tangled past that's not uncommon in LA. In the 1940s it was a Mexican American neighborhood, filled with residents who'd been unable to own homes elsewhere due to racist land covenants. Eyeing this prime land near downtown, the city declared it 'blighted' (it wasn't) and forced out homeowners, claiming the land would be used for public housing (it wasn't). Chavez Ravine was then bulldozed. In 1958 the land was given to Walter O'Malley, who broke a million Brooklyn hearts and moved the Dodgers to LA.

Best Places for...

$ Budget $$ Midrange $$$ Top End

See p72 for map of locations

Eating

People-Watching

Figaro Bistrot $$
9 B6

A culinary ménage à trois in Los Feliz involving a boulangerie, a bistro and a lounge, Figaro channels Paris with heavy mirrors, sidewalk tables and Gallic-inspired fare. The coffee crowd slowly morphs into a drinking crowd. *8am–midnight*

Black Cat $$
10 D6

Silver Lake site of a 1967 LGBTQ+ civil rights demonstration after a police raid during New Year's Eve celebrations. Today it's still a neighborhood hangout. Casual bar food is paired with good cocktails and fab people-watching. *4pm–2am*

Casual Bites

House of Pies $$
11 A5

Indomitable survivor of a chain that once swept California. Serves top diner fare like burgers, salads, chicken this and shrimp that. Of course, you're really here for its namesake desserts, which come in myriad flavors. *7am–1am*

Pazzo Gelato $
12 D6

Luscious Florence-style gelato in Silver Lake. If it's fresh at local farmers markets, it's likely a flavor here. The seasonal fresh-peach gelato is worth setting a calendar alert for; year-round flavors are worth trying one at a time. *10am–10pm*

Pine & Crane $$
13 E6

You'll be licking your chopsticks at this popular fast-casual spot in Silver Lake for small plates, noodles and rice-based dishes. Feast on spicy shrimp wontons, nutty *dan dan* noodles and the unmissable beef roll. *noon–10pm*

Playita Mariscos $
14 E7

Homemade tortillas and fresh seafood star at this simple Mexican cafe with a short menu. Plenty of seating outside. The menu consists of tacos, dorados, quesadillas and ceviche – and that's it. The authentic flavors extend to the cabbage (used instead of lettuce). *11am–9pm*

HomeState $
15 B8

A tasty ode to the Lone Star State in Los Feliz, where everyone queues patiently for authentic breakfast tacos and rustic Texan creations such as a brisket sandwich made with Mexican flair. Lots of shady outdoor seating. *7am–10pm*

Top Tables

Speranza $$
16 E4

Feels like a secret club in Silver Lake, but it's not – it's just sign-challenged; the verdant patio is the spot for traditional Italian fare like handmade pastas. This is the place to bring a date for a tête-à-tête. *5:30-11pm*

All Time 💲💲
 17 D4

Celebrates California produce and flavors in Los Feliz. Tuck into high-quality fare by day. Dinner features a short, market-driven menu featuring house-baked breads and seasonal fare. Lots of veggie options. *8am-10pm*

Drinking

Fun Bars

Tiki-Ti
18 D5

Channeling Waikiki in Los Feliz since 1961, this tiny tropical tavern packs in everyone from stylish slummers to 'non-ironic' partiers in Hawaiian shirts. Drinks are strong and smooth; most are served in comically themed collectibles. *6pm-midnight Wed-Sat*

Akbar
19 D6

Fun-loving, Casbah-style bar in Silver Lake that's diverse, attitude-free and a refreshing antidote to the look-at-me WeHo

scene. There's no shortage of theme nights, from live acts and karaoke to late-week dance sessions with renowned DJs. *4pm-2am*

Bartenders with Flair

Covell
20 B7

Over 150 wines by the glass in Los Feliz. Lovely lounge showcases interesting producers, unusual grapes and lesser-known regions. Barkeeps are knowledgeable and generous with tastings. Seasonal, tapas-style bites are gorgeous, with creative concepts and presentation. *4pm-midnight*

Ototo
21 F8

Japanese craft-beer bar in Echo Park is big with Dodgers fans pre-game, who then walk to the stadium. Intimate; pours a rotating selection of Japanese rice wines, categorized by flavor profile. Great snacks; vaunted Tsubaki restaurant adjoins. *5-10pm*

Places to Hang

Bar Flores
see **21** F8

Upstairs Echo Park cantina faces Sunset

Blvd; views of the 'hood, with a glow provided by candles. Mellow vibe encourages long evenings with friends, made all the better with delicious drinks and snacks. *4pm-2am*

Eightfold Coffee
see **21** F8

Stylists and musicians flock to this minimalist, whitewashed coffee shop to talk gigs, browse niche journals and sip superlative coffee. Decent pastries and bites. *7:30am-4pm*

Shopping

Eclectic

Wacko
22 B7

A sprawling Los Feliz carnival of pop, kitsch and camp is always a fun browse. Pick up a *Star Wars* tote or a latex unicorn mask. The 'Build your own conspiracy' kit is a top seller. *11am-7pm*

Time Travel Mart
23 F8

Indescribable Echo Park shop. Goods all have some relationship to time, whether it's a book about dinosaurs titled *All My Friends Are Still Dead* or 'Alternative Universe' keychains. The store's slogan is: 'Whenever you are, we're already there.' *noon-6pm*

Market

Silver Lake Farmers Market
24 D6

The best locally sourced produce, prepared foods and artisan coffee, treats, vintage clothing and more for a demanding crowd. *1:30-7pm Tue, 6am-1:30pm Sat*

Clothing

Kingswell
25 B6

Los Feliz skate shop is one of SoCal's best. Custom boards, gear and art exhibits. Has its own line of clothing, and the staff are all skateboarders and share a wealth of info with customers. *noon-6pm*

Matrushka Construction
26 D7

Writers, film-industry types and indie style queens love this Silver Lake boutique and work-shop run by designer Lara Howe. The frocks, jumpsuits, leggings and more are all made in LA using bold, vintage-inspired fabrics. *hours vary*

Luxe De Ville
27 F8

Echo Park's Oskar de la Cruz has a sharp eye for rare vintage threads, whether it's a Lillie Rubin frock, a vintage ostrich coat or a 1960s mod-style hat. He also collaborates on custom wear. *noon-7pm*

Lemon Frog
28 F8

Bold, vibrant patterns and colors dominate at this jam-packed treasure trove of vintage fashion. Look for more sought-after goods deeper in the store. Duds span the '60s to the 2000s. *11am-3pm*

Books & Tunes

Skylight Books
29 B6

Bifurcated Los Feliz institution carries everything from art, architecture and fashion tomes to LA history titles, vegan cookbooks, queer literature and critical theory. There are fun lit-themed tees

and regular, engaging in-store readings and talks. Great staff picks. *10am-10pm*

Stories
see **23** F8

Score anything and everything from plays, poetry and short-story anthologies to graphic novels, brain-twisting metaphysics titles and LA-themed books. Brainy types congregate in the back-end cafe, which comes with a cute back patio. *9am-9pm*

Reverie Bookstand
see **21** F8

Find treasures from used Joyce to *Michael Chekhov's Acting Technique* at this gem of an Echo Park bookstore. The offerings are limited, but they're carefully curated. The entire shop is a staff recommendation. *11am-7pm*

Sick City Records
see **21** F8

Get your punk groove on at this used-album shop with rare finds in Echo Park. Prowl the bins for treasures turned in from local luminaries thinning out their collections. *1-7pm Tue-Sun*

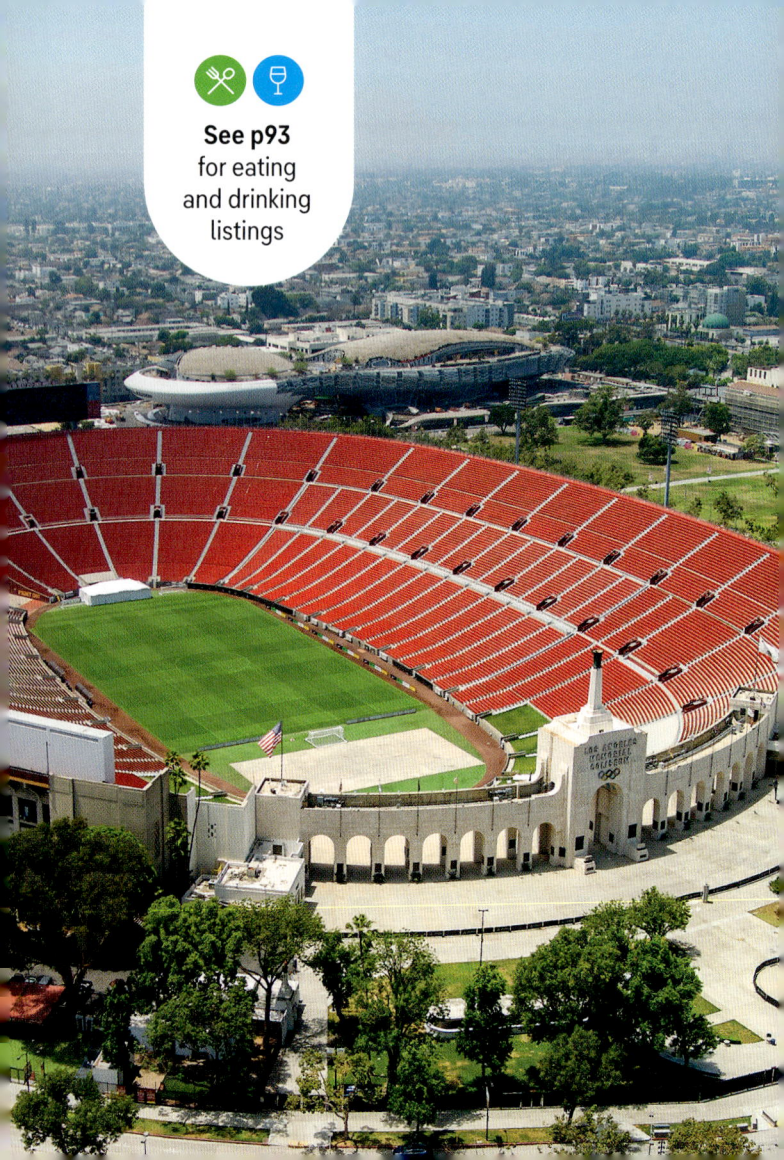

See p93
for eating
and drinking
listings

Explore
Exposition Park & South LA

The massive area south of the Santa Monica Fwy (I-10) and straddling the Harbor Fwy (I-110) comprises dozens of neighborhoods collectively called South LA. At its northern end are Exposition Park, home to LA's iconic Memorial Coliseum, popular museums and the University of Southern California (USC).

A couple of miles west, Leimert Park is the thriving, beating heart of LA's African American community, and east of I-110 is Watts, known for Watts Towers, a masterpiece of folk art. South LA burst into the global consciousness with some of hip-hop's greatest pioneers, such as Ice-T, Ice Cube and, later, Tupac Shakur.

Getting Around

 Metro
The Metro Rail E Line has stops at Expo Park. There's also a DASH bus route from Downtown (50¢). The A Line serves Compton and Watts. The K Line serves Downtown Inglewood and the LAX area.

 Car
South LA is the stereotypical SoCal sprawl of suburbia. You'll need a car to get around. None of the privately built stadiums in the SoFi Stadium area are located near mass transit. Expo Park is the one ideal place for extended walking.

Aerial view of Los Angeles Memorial Coliseum (p91)
MARCUS E JONES/SHUTTERSTOCK

THE BEST

FAMOUS LOCATION
Los Angeles Memorial Coliseum (p91)

FOLK ART
Watts Towers (p92)

NIGHT OUT
Somerville (p93)

ART EXHIBIT CAAM (p91)

MEMORABLE BITE
Randy's Donuts (p93)

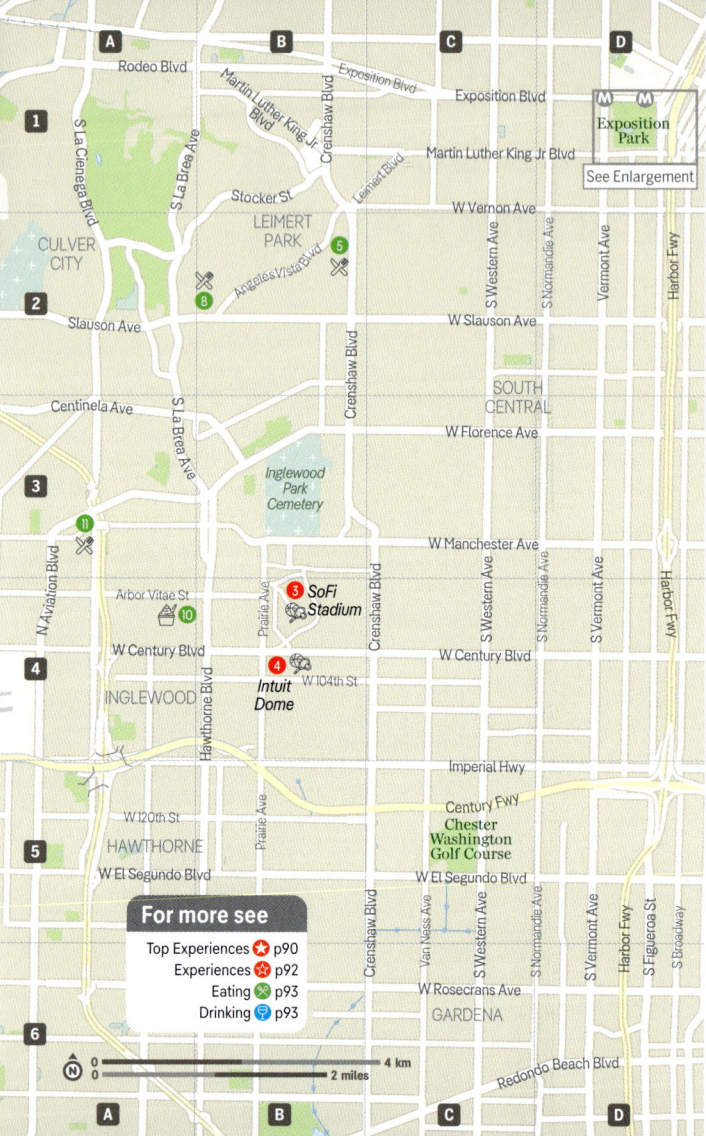

Rodeo Blvd

Exposition Blvd

Exposition Blvd

1

S La Cienega Blvd

S La Brea Ave

Martin Luther King Jr Blvd

Crenshaw Blvd

M M

Exposition Park

See Enlargement

Martin Luther King Jr Blvd

Stocker St

W Vernon Ave

LEIMERT PARK

S Western Ave

S Normandie Ave

Vermont Ave

Harbor Fwy

5

CULVER CITY

Angeles Vista Blvd

Leimert Blvd

8

2

Slauson Ave

W Slauson Ave

Centinela Ave

S La Brea Ave

Crenshaw Blvd

SOUTH CENTRAL

W Florence Ave

3

Inglewood Park Cemetery

11

W Manchester Ave

N Aviation Blvd

Arbor Vitae St

S Western Ave

S Normandie Ave

S Vermont Ave

Harbor Fwy

10

Prairie Ave

3 *SoFi Stadium*

Crenshaw Blvd

4

W Century Blvd

Intuit Dome

W 104th St

W Century Blvd

Hawthorne Blvd

INGLEWOOD

Imperial Hwy

Century Fwy

5

W 120th St

Prairie Ave

HAWTHORNE

Chester Washington Golf Course

W El Segundo Blvd

W El Segundo Blvd

S Figueroa St

S Broadway

Harbor Fwy

S Vermont Ave

S Normandie Ave

S Western Ave

Van Ness Ave

Crenshaw Blvd

For more see

Top Experiences ⭐ p90
Experiences 🌟 p92
Eating ✖ p93
Drinking 🔵 p93

W Rosecrans Ave

GARDENA

6

N

0   4 km
0   2 miles

Redondo Beach Blvd

A   B   C   D

University of Southern California

Exposition Blvd

M Expo Park/USC

M Expo/ Vermont

Natural History Museum

California Science Center

CAAM

State Dr

Kinsey Dr

N Coliseum Dr

Exposition Park

W 39th St

Vermont Ave

Bill Robertson La

Los Angeles Memorial Coliseum

S Coliseum Dr

S Figueroa St

Flower Dr

Harbor Fwy

S Flower St

W 37th St

9

S Grand Ave

S Hill St

W 39th St

S Broadway

BMO Stadium

S Park Dr

Martin Luther King Jr Blvd

0 — 500 m
0 — 0.25 miles

E Jefferson Blvd

E Broadway

E Vernon Ave

E Slauson Ave

E Florence Ave

Florence Ave

FLORENCE

Compton Ave

Nadeau St

State St

California Ave

Otis St

Atlantic Ave

E Manchester Ave

Avalon Blvd

S Central Ave

S Alameda St

Long Beach Blvd

Firestone Blvd

E Century Blvd

Tweedy Blvd

South Gate Park

GREEN MEADOWS

Watts Towers

1

Compton Ave

Santa Ana Blvd

SOUTH GATE

Martin Luther King Jr Blvd

Long Beach Fwy

Imperial Hwy

Imperial Hwy

Los Angeles River

Century Fwy

E El Segundo Blvd

S Avalon Blvd

S Central Ave

E El Segundo Blvd

N Washington Ave

S Alameda St

Santa Fe Ave

Long Beach Blvd

Century Fwy

Atlantic Ave

COMPTON

W Rosecrans Ave

E Rosecrans Ave

S Avalon Blvd

W Compton Blvd

12

E Compton Blvd

Somerset Blvd

7 2 **Martin Luther King Memorial**

6

W Alondra Blvd

E Alondra Blvd

E

F

G

H

Tour Expo Park on Foot

Expo Park's major attractions are obvious (three major museums with another coming someday, plus a huge coliseum). But the historic 160-acre site holds a lot more. The Rose Garden alone is one of LA's most popular attractions, and as you're strolling, there are discoveries that tell you more about the region as a whole.

START	END	LENGTH
Rose Garden	Lucas Museum of Narrative Art	1 mile; 2 hours

1 Garden of Roses

Your first whiff of Expo Park when you exit the E Train is sweet. The stately **Rose Garden** fronting the Expo Park/USC station covers 7 acres and is planted with over 15,000 rose bushes in just about every color nature can provide. This one garden sees over a million visitors a year, including bridal parties, prom couples and families in search of the perfect group shot.

2 Plane Parked

Angle east and you'll soon see a large United Airlines **DC-8 airliner**. Built at the former Douglas Aircraft plant in Long Beach in 1966, it flew in and out of LAX for nearly 20 years and is a good representative of a time when Los Angeles County was home to two of the world's then three major commercial airliner manufacturers (Douglas and Lockheed), with only Boeing elsewhere (Washington).

3 LA's Spacecraft

Follow along the front of the **CAAM** (p91), and stop in to see what's on. To your right, the soaring new Samuel Oschin Air and Space Center at the **California Science Center** (p90) will house several famous products of LA County's once ubiquitous aerospace industry. These include the space shuttle *Endeavour* (Palmdale) and an Apollo Command Module (Downey), like the kind that went to the moon.

4 Burbank Speedster

Just past the Oschin site, the black, arrow-shaped plane is yet another LA County product. In the 'your tax dollars at work' category, the **A-12** was a top-secret 1960s CIA spy plane built by Lockheed in Burbank. Able to fly at an astonishing Mach 3.3, the plane was meant to take spy pics of the Soviet Union. However, satellites superseded it before it did much.

5 Beware of Genitalia

Head to the entrance of the Memorial Coliseum. Look for the two 25ft-high naked bronze figures on the **Olympic Gateway** to the stadium near the Olympic rings. Designed by artist Robert Graham for the 1984 games, the figures' nakedness caused concern, with President Ronald Reagan suggesting the equivalent of togas be added (which didn't happen).

6 Museum of Mystery

Past the Coliseum, the enormous, sinuous blob rising west of the Coliseum is the **Lucas Museum of Narrative Art** (*lucasmuseum. org*). The dream of George Lucas, creator of *Star Wars*, the huge metallic shell will hold a museum 'to inspire and connect people through the exploration of visual stories and their influences in society.' Amid years of missed deadlines and hundreds of millions spent, few know what that really means.

★ **TOP EXPERIENCE**

Exposition Park

Exposition Park – or **Expo Park** – began as an agricultural fairground in 1872, emerging as a patch of public greenery in 1913. Then Los Angeles Memorial Coliseum came along and, in the next century, three major museums (and soon a fourth), two summer Olympics and many more sporting events, including another Olympics in 2028.

MAP P86 **G2**

PLANNING TIP
Metro Rail's Expo Park/USC stop on the E Line puts you right at the Rose Garden at the center of Exposition Park. Downtown is only 10 minutes away.

Scan this QR code for full details on the attractions and events at Expo Park.

Shuttle & Science

The crowd-pleasing favorite in Expo Park, the **California Science Center** *(californiasciencecenter.org; free)* remains open even as the enormous new Samuel Oschin Air and Space Center is added. Sometime after 2026 this soaring new wing will show off the museum's pride and joy, the space shuttle *Endeavour*, one of only three existing shuttles to go into space. It will be shown ready for launch with its rockets and the external fuel tank attached. In the meantime, popular exhibits include a simulated earthquake and the World of Life, focusing on the five life processes that unite living creatures from single-cell amoebae to we, 100-trillion-cell humans.

Natural History Museum

From dinos to diamonds, the **Natural History Museum** *(nhm.org; adult/child $18/7; pictured right)* takes you around the world and through eons. A new wing, NHM Commons, opens up the interior to the 3.5-acre gardens, with over 600 plant species.

Among the features is **Gnatalie**, a long-necked 70ft-long dinosaur. It's all housed in a beautiful 1913 Spanish Renaissance–style building that stood in for Columbia University, where Peter Parker was bitten by the radioactive arachnid, in the first Tobey Maguire *Spider-Man* movie.

LEE HARI/SHUTTERSTOCK

California's African American Museum

Showcasing the works of African American artists, **CAAM** *(California African American Museum; caamuseum.org; free)* focuses on the African American experience in California and LA. The five galleries feature only changing exhibitions. Some feature big names such as folk artist Nellie Mae Rowe.

Los Angeles Coliseum

The centerpiece here is the grand, 77,500-seat 1923 **Los Angeles Memorial Coliseum** *(lacoliseum.com)*. It hosted the 1932 and 1984 Olympic Games, and will be a venue for the 2028 Games. It has also hosted Super Bowls, NFL, a World Series (1959) and, since 1923, the USC Trojans football team. Plus, it's been the site of famous speeches and other special events. **Guided tours** *(adult/child $28/22)* are offered.

QUICK BREAK
A five-minute walk from Expo Park under the I-110 freeway, the fabulous food hall **Mercado La Paloma** (p93) has a dozen stalls selling everything from Yucatán cuisine to Thai.

EXPERIENCES

Marvel at Watts Towers
PUBLIC FOLK ART

MAP: **1** P86 **F4**

The three 'Gothic' (or is it Gaudí-esque?) spires of the fabulous **Watts Towers** (*wattstowers. org; tour adult/child $7/3*) rank among the world's greatest monuments of folk art. In 1921, Italian immigrant Simon Rodia set out to 'make something big' and then spent 33 years cobbling together this whimsical free-form sculpture from concrete, steel and a motley assortment of found objects, from green 7 Up bottles to seashells, tiles, rocks and pottery.

The towers reach up to 99.5ft in height, just below the city's legal limit of 100ft. You can admire Watts Towers from beyond the fence 24/7 (and there's good explanatory signage), but to get inside you must take the tour.

The adjacent **Watts Towers Art Center** has rotating exhibitions by important artists such as David G Brown's searing political cartoons. The campus is a short walk from the Metro Rail A Line 103rd St/Watts Towers station.

Compton's Anthem Location
MUSIC VIDEO LOCATION

MAP: **2** P86 **F6**

Compton remains relevant musically, as megastar Kendrick Lamar showed in 2024 with his music video 'Not Like Us.' Viewed millions of times, it features scenes shot at the striking modernist **Martin Luther King Memorial** on the wide open plaza at the Compton City Hall.

Lamar invited Compton to show up for the shoot, and they did. The results are joyous and vivacious. Watch the video on your phone while you visit.

SoFi & Intuit
STADIUMS

Flying into LAX, you'll likely spot the new and growing complex of corporate-financed stadiums east of the airport in Inglewood. Largest is **SoFi Stadium** (MAP: **3** P86 **B4**; *sofistadium.com*), a huge, flashy NFL stadium that some would say has a split personality and others would say has no personality. That's because the 70,200-seat arena serves two teams, the LA Rams and the LA Chargers, and can't show allegiance to either.

Just south, past a growing mall, the glitzy **Intuit Dome** (MAP: **4** P86 **B4**; Intuit makes tax prep apps; *intuitdome.com*) puts on a nighttime light show and is home to the NBA's LA Clippers.

See p86 for map of locations

EXPLORE

EXPOSITION PARK & SOUTH LA

Best Places for...

$** Budget   **$$** Midrange   **$$$ Top End

Eating

Top Meals

Dulan's On Crenshaw $$

5 B2

Near Leimert Park, this soul food mainstay serves classic dishes in a lovely, designer space. A photo of the owner's grandparents, noted LA restaurateurs, overlooks the dining room. Great mac and cheese. *11am-8pm*

Kitchen's Corner $$

6 H6

This top Compton food truck is so popular that it's double the typical size. The Texas-style fall-off-the-bone barbecue is a succulent treat and keeps repeat business booming. Enjoy the takeaway servings at the big park across Atlantic Ave. *11am-7pm*

Alma's Place $$

7 F6

Near Compton City Hall, Alma cooks 'food for the soul.' The restaurant is no-nonsense, but that's fine as all the atmosphere comes from the good cheer and the splendid specials, like her pork chops and catfish. *11am-5pm*

Somerville $$

8 B2

Swank Slauson Ave spot evoking a 1940s supper club. Elegance is the theme here, where soul meets steakhouse. Cool jazz plays, setting the vibe. Always a hot table; book well ahead and plan to dress. *6-11pm Wed-Sun*

Quick Eats

Mercado La Paloma $

9 H1

A quick walk under I-110 from Expo Park, this fabulous food hall has everything your heart could desire. A great breeding ground for inventive chefs. Wander the aisles and see what takes your fancy. *9am-9pm*

Foster's Freeze $

10 A4

Time-warp Inglewood soft-serve ice-cream emporium that hasn't changed in decades – good! Order a hot fudge sundae with the thick, gooey topping sliding down the creamy novelty and enjoy it at a picnic table. Savory snacks, too. *10am-8pm*

Randy's Donuts $

11 A3

Famously excellent doughnuts are your first or last memory of LA, going to or from LAX. Sure, there are social-media variations, but the simplest of flavors, like glazed old-fashioned, are the best. *24/7*

Drinking

Specialty Coffee

Patria Coffee Roasters

12 G6

Only a block from Compton's City Hall and next to a park, this art-filled coffee house is a standout for top-end coffee drinks. It's a real antidote to generic chains. Beverages are served with Compton pride. *8am-3pm*

for eating,
drinking and
shopping
listings

Explore
Pasadena & Highland Park

Researched by
Ryan Ver Berkmoes

In Pasadena, you'll find a community with an old-money soul, a historical perspective, an appreciation for art and jazz, an old-school conservative undercurrent and a reverence for tradition. The Rose Bowl college football game dates to 1916, the namesake stadium opened in 1923 and the Rose Parade that perfumes the streets began in 1890.

Highland Park is not a place to tick off big-ticket sights. Its walkable, low-rise streets are a hub of cool cafes, bars and boutiques, all living next to throwback old-school faves. Figueroa St has a long strip of interesting places, and there's another cluster on York Blvd near Ave 50.

Getting Around

Metro
The Metro Rail A Line serves Pasadena and Highland Park, connecting both to Downtown and beyond. Pasadena stations are at the western and northern edges of Downtown. The Huntington is not near transit; you'll need a rideshare from a transit stop. Highland Park station lies one block behind one of the two main drags, N Figueroa St.

Bus
Metro Bus Line 662 serves the Rose Bowl. Metro bus 182 runs along N Figueroa St and York Blvd in Highland Park.

THE BEST

DAY OUT
Huntington (p100)

ICE CREAM Scoops (p103)

THEATRE Pasadena
Playhouse (p102)

BOOKSTORE
Vroman's (p105)

BAR WITH MUSIC
Gold Line (p104)

Pasadena Playhouse (p102)

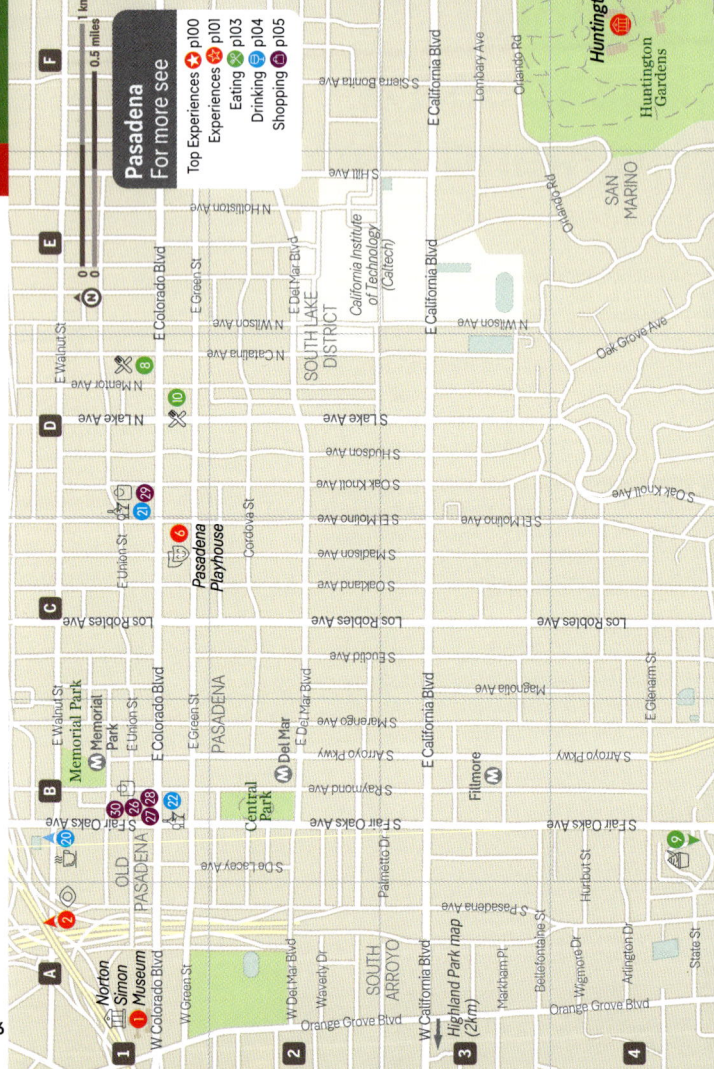

Pasadena
For more see

Top Experiences p100
Experiences p101
Eating p103
Drinking p104
Shopping p105

Huntington

Huntington
Gardens

SAN
MARINO

California Institute
of Technology
(Caltech)

SOUTH LAKE
DISTRICT

Pasadena
Playhouse

PASADENA

Memorial
Park

Central
Park

OLD
PASADENA

Norton
Simon
Museum

SOUTH
ARROYO

Highland Park map
(2km)

1 km

0.5 miles

N Figueroa St

Pasadena map
(2mi)

Newland St

N Figueroa St

Roy St

Meridian St

Branch St

York Blvd

Aldama St

Los Angeles
Police
Museum 3

HIGHLAND
PARK

Mesa Ave

Outlook Ave

12

Highland
Park

33

16

Fayette St

York Blvd

Galco's
Old World
Grocery 5

N Ave 52

Nolden St

Baltimore St

Hub St

N Ave 51

Ash St

N High Dr

N Ave 50

Highland
Park

M

25

4

24

17

Highland
Park
Bowl

Meridian St

Rangeview Ave

Meridian St

N Ave 55

N Ave 54

N Ave 53

Irvington Pl

Aldama St

Monte Vista Dr

31

Hammond St

11

Rangeview Ave

Stratford Rd

Meridian St

York Blvd

N Ave 51

Lincoln Ave

Buchanan St

Baltimore St

N Ave 53

Avenue 53

N Ave 50

Holland Ave

N Ave 50

Bob Baker
Marionette
Theater

14 13 32

15

34 35

18

7

23

19

EAGLE
ROCK

Campus Rd

Lincoln Ave

Buchanan St

Baltimore St

York Blvd

Arrindale Ave

El Paso Dr

Tce 49

Cresta Ave

Highland Park
For more see

Experiences p101
Eating p103
Drinking p104
Shopping p105

0.5 km
0.25 miles

WALKING TOUR

Walking Pasadena

Pasadena is imbued with old-school Americana. It has a certain genteel comfort that you'll sense along its immaculate streets, where gnarled oaks shade gracious arts-and-crafts mansions. Color comes from top museums and Old Pasadena, a lively 20-block shopping and entertainment district of historic brick buildings.

START	END	LENGTH
Rose Bowl Stadium	Pasadena Playhouse	3.25 miles; 3 hours

1 At the Rose Bowl

The venerable 1922 **Rose Bowl Stadium** seats up to 92,500 spectators and shines every New Year's when it hosts the Rose Bowl post-season college football game. The second Sunday of every month, one of the world's largest flea markets *(rgcshows.com)* is held here. Surrounding Brookside Park offers hiking, cycling and picnicking. Families can check out the excellent Kidspace Children's Museum *(kidspacemuseum.org; $15.50).*

2 Gamble's Masterpiece

Follow Rosemont Ave to exquisite **Gamble House** *(gamblehouse. org; adult/child $20/free).* The 1908 masterpiece of Craftsman architecture was built for David Gamble, heir to Procter & Gamble (Tide, Crest etc). Incorporating 17 types of wood, art glass and subdued light, the entire home is a work of art, with its foundation, furniture and fixtures united by a common design.

3 Top Art Museum

Rodin's *The Thinker* is only a taste of the bounty of art at the exquisite **Norton Simon Museum** (p101). On this walk, concentrate on the gardens, which feature Western sculpture and are inspired by Monet's garden at Giverny. Recent work on the museum's exterior and grounds has revitalized the 115,000 glazed tiles, plantings and water features. Head east on Colorado Blvd.

4 Strolling Old Pasadena

Old Pasadena is the visitor-friendly heart of downtown Pasadena. In streets lined with century-old brick buildings are all kinds of shops and places to eat and drink. Some are upscale chains; others are locally owned; and some are delightfully idiosyncratic, such as Gold Bug (p105), which features collections by 100 area designers and artists. For a coffee, try Copa Vida.

5 Discoveries at the Pacific Asia Museum

In a 1920s Chinese Imperial Palace–style building, the **USC Pacific Asia Museum** *(pacificasiamuseum.usc.edu; adult/ child $20/free)* has a deep collection of Japanese paintings, some dating back to the 17th century and the Edo Meiji period. Other works include illustrations, Buddhist and Hindu masterpieces and Chinese ceramics. Exhibits explore Asian American culture and the links between the two continents.

6 A Night of Drama

Sample fine California cuisine at the art deco–inspired Bistro 45 (p103), then make an evening of it with a show at the **Pasadena Playhouse** (p102), the landmark theater that's trained two generations of well-known actors. Wander around the building's exterior Spanish Revival passages, where you'll find various plaques and honors accumulated over its more than 100 years of staging important works.

⭐ **TOP EXPERIENCE**

The Huntington

Utterly unmissable, the **Huntington** is a highlight of any trip to California, thanks to its world-class mix of art, literary history and over 120 acres of themed gardens (any one of which would be worth a visit on its own), all set amid stately grounds.

MAP P96 **F4**

PLANNING TIP
Start at the Orientation Gallery, where you can try to prioritize your visit. Pick up the laughably misnamed 'I have an hour tour' guide, which takes at least two hours.

Scan this QR code for full opening hours and to book ahead.

Printed Treasures

There's so much to see and do that it's hard to know where to begin; allow three to four hours for even a basic visit. Be sure to book ahead at busy times.

The **library** is a good place to get a sense of the Huntington's treasures. Only a fraction of the six million rare books are on display at any time, but the highlights are impressive: a Gutenberg Bible, a manuscript of *The Canterbury Tales* by Geoffrey Chaucer, plus a copy of Marco Polo's book about his travels with annotations by Christopher Columbus.

Masterpieces

In the **galleries** of European and American art you can lose yourself in the brushstrokes of Thomas Gainsborough's *The Blue Boy* and Thomas Lawrence's *Pinkie*. Other artists here include Mary Cassatt, Edward Hopper, Andy Warhol and Frank Stella.

Note the dour portraits of the patrons, Henry and Arabella Huntington. They partly made their fortune by owning the 'Red Cars,' the trolley system that stitched the LA region together 100 years ago (which is now being partly reconstituted).

Gardens & More Gardens

The extensive **gardens** – about a dozen – are as carefully curated as the museums themselves. Don't miss the roses, the Chinese Garden, the Japanese Garden and the lush Jungle Garden.

EXPERIENCES

Be Dazzled by the
Norton Simon Museum   ART MUSEUM

MAP: **1** P96 **A1**

Rodin's *The Burghers of Calais* and *The Thinker* near the entrance are only an overture to the symphony of art in store at Pasadena's exquisite **Norton Simon Museum** *(nortonsimon.org; adult/child $20/free)*. Norton Simon (1907–93) was an entrepreneur with a passion for art who parlayed his fortune into a remarkable collection.

The galleries teem with works by Renaissance and impressionist artists, including Rembrandt *(Self-Portrait)*, Renoir *(Young Woman in Black)*, Canaletto *(Piazzetta in Venice Looking North)* and Van Gogh, as well as an outstanding array by Degas. The 20th century masterpieces span Picasso and LA's own Sam Francis.

Asian sculpture – principally Buddhist and Hindu imagery in stone, bronze and copper – is another high point. The **sculpture garden**, inspired by Monet's in Giverny, is superb. A massive revamp of the grounds began in 2025.

Discover the
Cosmos at JPL   SCIENCE LABS

MAP: **2** P96 **A1**

The world's premier space-exploration agency, the **Jet Propulsion Laboratory** *(JPL; jpl.nasa.gov; free)* has commanded robot explorers on Mars and interplanetary probes leaving our solar system from this campus on the northern side of Pasadena.

The accomplishments of the scientists and engineers here, working in conjunction with CalTech and, at times, international space agencies, are extraordinary. And it's all done with cool professionalism and a lack of bombast or over-hyped claims. Fascinating **tours** of the facility that birthed the Mars rovers and that is plotting the first ever return of Martian soil – among other feats – can be arranged at least three weeks ahead via the website.

Visit LA's
Police Museum   MUSEUM

MAP: **3** P97 **F2**

Crime fighting (with a dose of TV cop Jack Webb) is in the spotlight at Highland Park's Police Station No 11 (1926), now repurposed as the **Los Angeles Police Museum** *(laphs.org; adult/child $10/5)*. Exhibits trace the history of the LAPD from its humble beginnings in 1869 to the modern force of today. There's fascinating background on some of the city's most notorious crimes, but don't expect much on the department's many controversies.

Score a Strike at Highland
Park Bowl   HISTORIC BOWLING ALLEY

MAP: **4** P97 **E4**

You won't find a bowling alley as stunningly original as the 1927 **Highland Park Bowl** *(highlandparkbowl.com)*. Its steampunk fit-out includes upcycled pinsetters-turned-chandeliers, leather Chesterfield sofas and twin bars serving rotating craft cocktails and beers.

Taste Old World Candy & Soda
SPECIALTY GROCERY STORE

MAP: **5** P97 **E2**

You'll find over 700 small-batch and heritage sodas at Highland Park's family-run **Galco's Old World Grocery** *(sodapopstop. com)*, from botanically brewed British cola to legacy brands such as Frostie blue cream soda. You can even make your own using flavors such as toasted marshmallow and huckleberry. Heighten the sugar rush with some old-school candy (gotta love the Necco wafers!).

Note: the Idaho Spud candy bar is an acquired taste.

Watch Top Plays at Pasadena Playhouse
THEATER

MAP: **6** P96 **C1**

Fully deserving of the word 'legend,' the **Pasadena Playhouse** *(pasadenaplayhouse.org)*, an attractive Spanish Colonial complex, was founded in 1917, and by 1937 had developed such a reputation that it was named State Theater of California. It ran a lauded acting school in the 1930s and 1940s and has premiered hundreds of works. Grads include Dustin Hoffman, Gene Hackman

and Leonard Nimoy. It won the Tony Award in 2023 for best regional theater in the US.

Smile with the Puppets
PUPPET THEATER

MAP: **7** P97 **B1**

A former vaudeville theater in Highland Park is home to the much-loved **Bob Baker Marionette Theater** *(bobbaker marionettetheater.com),* LA's oldest children's theater company. The cast includes over 2000 puppets, some from the 1940s. It has fans of all ages. The troupe's guiding principle is sweetness in its productions.

PASADENA'S ROSE PARADE
Presented annually since 1890, the **Tournament of Roses Parade** *(tournamentofroses.com)* runs for 5.5 miles along Colorado Blvd through downtown Pasadena. The highlight: floats masterfully decorated entirely with flowers and plant material, from seeds to fruit to fronds. Can't make it to the parade? Check out these remarkable works at the **Showcase of Floats** for a couple of days after the parade.

The parade runs every January 1, unless that's a Sunday, in which case it goes until January 2. Now that the Rose Bowl football game is part of the college football playoffs, it can take place as much as a week after the parade.

LISTINGS

Best Places for...

$** Budget   **$$** Midrange   **$$$ Top End

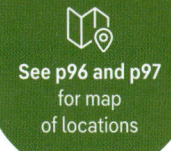

See p96 and p97
for map
of locations

Eating

Good Eating in Pasadena

Artisanal Goods by CAR $
8 P96 **D1**

The best $6 chocolate croissant you'll ever eat. Countless curvaceous layers wrapped around a succulent filling. Sit inside or at a sidewalk table. Cafe does other treats and coffee. *8:30am-5pm Tue-Sun*

Fair Oaks Pharmacy $
9 P96 **B4**

Nostalgic 1915 ice-cream fountain where 'soda jerks' dish out 'phosphates' (flavored syrup and soda water), banana splits, malts, sundaes and any other treat you can conjure up. *9am-5pm Mon-Sat*

Bistro 45 $$$
10 P96 **D1**

Sample fine California cuisine with French accents in an art deco–inspired dining room. Elegant yet not stiff, with the best local ingredients. If it's warm, Pasadena's best tables are on the patio. *5-8:30pm Tue-Sun*

Casual Eats in Highland Park

Villa's Tacos $
11 P97 **D4**

Tucked into the corner of a strip mall, Villa's serves award-winning Mexican fare. Order the Villas Trio, three tacos that combine veggie, chorizo and pork options. The salsa bar is sublime, especially the mango habanero. *noon-10pm*

Mariscos El Faro $
12 P97 **F3**

Popular seafood-centric food truck serving *empanadas de camaron:* a tortilla stuffed with cheese, shrimp and onions and then deep-fried until crispy. Take your plate to adjoining Highland Park for a picnic. *10am-6pm*

Donut Friend $
13 P97 **C1**

Don't miss the wildly creative deep-fried treats, sprinkled with such esoteric choices as coconut bacon, or made with bananas or drizzled in glazes such as matcha tea and maple. Fresh raspberries as toppings are sublime. *7am-9pm*

Scoops $
14 P97 **C1**

Neighbor to Donut Friend, this small shop serves small-batch ice cream, offered in out-of-the-box flavors like matcha horchata Oreo. Don't put too much stock in the names: a perennial favorite is 'brown bread.' *2-9pm*

Joy $
15 P97 **C1**

Casual eatery whipping up brilliance. Snap at plump wontons, flavor-packed mapo tofu and crunchy thousand-layer pancakes, best jacked up with chili sauce, basil, cheese and egg. The scallion bread sandwiches are divine. *noon-10pm*

Kitchen Mouse Cafe $
16 P97 **E4**

Adorned with fresh flowers and sidewalk

tables, this veggie cafe draws loyal fans for large portions of inventive seasonal fare. A big fave: the avocado TLT, with avocado, maple-tempeh bacon, cherry tomatoes and aioli. *8am-4pm*

Highland Park Restaurants for a Night Out

Checker Hall 🟢🟢

 17 P97 **D4**

Med meals are served upstairs in the heart of the Figueroa nightlife district. Lots of sharables and veggie options. Tables on a vintage porch. Inside is a plush elegance that cries 'date night.' Music leans romantic. *5-10pm*

Belle's 🟢🟢

18 P97 **B1**

Leading the transition of the York Blvd strip from a haven for reupholstery shops to on-trend neighborhood hangouts. Great bagels in the morning, more ambitious fare later in the day. Full bar and an open front. *7am-10pm Wed-Mon*

Queen St Raw Bar & Grill 🟢🟢🟢

19 P97 **A1**

Raw oysters and grilled fish stream from the kitchen at this popular bistro with an old

waterfront vibe. Sit at the marble-topped horseshoe bar or reserve a table on the quiet plaza. *5-10pm*

Drinking

Pasadena Drinking Spots

Highlight Coffee

20 P96 **B1**

Some of LA's best coffee, served by amazing staff in an unpretentious setting. The curated list of pour-over coffees is highly recommended, but the coffee lemonade is also really good. *7am-3pm*

1894

21 P96 **D1**

Excellent wine bar adjoining Vroman's Bookstore, with literary-themed cocktails, microbrews and an excellent selection of California wines. Creative savory and sweet snacks. *3-9pm Wed-Sun*

Lucky Baldwin's

22 P96 **B1**

English-style pub that pours dozens of English, Irish and American beers on tap in a woody warren of rooms. Or opt for the tables outside facing a small park. Yes, there's fish and chips. *midnight-11pm*

Highland Park Drinking Spots

Kumquat Coffee Co

23 P97 **B1**

Welcoming, minimalist space brewing superb coffee with meticulous attention to detail and local and international roasts. More unusual options include a popular hojicha (green tea) latte. Good pastries. *7am-5pm*

Gold Line

24 P97 **E4**

Vinyl is king at mellow hi-fi bar Gold Line. Its hefty record collection (over 8000) with rare discs from bar co-founder Peanut Butter Wolf lines the walls. Superb drinks. One of several good nightspots on Figueroa. *5pm-2am*

Lodge Room

see **17** P97 **D4**

Sweaty bar with regular live bands that draws crowds from across LA. Noted for being intimate, upstairs and having great sound. *hours vary*

Good Housekeeping

25 **E4**

Red-brick speakeasy and neighborly oasis of tea lights, leather booths and competent barkeeps. On-point cocktails favor quality spirits and ingredients. Good all-rounder. *6pm-1am*

Shopping

Pasadena Shops

Gold Bug
26 P96 **B1**

Amazing boutique with a steampunk vibe. Shows work and collections created by over 100 area artists. Exquisite vintage jewelry, build-your-own butterfly kits, steampunk gizmos and much more. *11am-5pm Thu-Mon*

Lather
27 P96 **B1**

Pasadena-based body-care products maker showcasing natural hand creams, exfoliants and other treatments at its flagship store. *10am-8pm*

Neo 39
28 P96 **B1**

In the Old Town Pasadena shopping district, this sneaker depot stocks rare, imported and stylish high tops, low tops and new releases. *noon-6pm Wed-Sun*

Vroman's Bookstore
29 P96 **D1**

Vroman's (founded 1894) claims to be the largest and oldest bookstore in SoCal. Huge selection, and regular events featuring top authors and readings. It's the kind of store where you can lose a few hours browsing. *10am-9pm*

Homage
30 P96 **B1**

A Pasadena treasure with a selection of gifts, stationery, jewelry, accessories and more that includes many locally designed items. One section is devoted to social causes. *11am-6pm*

Highland Park Shops

On Maritime Records
31 P97 **D4**

As shipshape and clean-lined as a racing yacht, this used-record store has a wonderfully curated selection of vinyl. Staff love to share recommendations. Known for rare finds and good prices. *noon-8pm*

Aroyo Records
32 P97 **C1**

Great old-school storefront with new and used LPs. The owner carefully manages the stock to keep it varied. Plan on searching the bins for a while. Surprising $1 specials. *noon-8pm*

North Figueroa Bookshop
33 P97 **F4**

Sets the standard for what a neighborhood bookstore should be. Sublime selection, engaging staff, regular events and more. *11am-7pm*

Big Bud Press
34 P97 **B1**

At the end of the rainbow lies this explosion of Technicolor grooviness. Designed and made in LA, its size-inclusive, unisex booty includes '70s-inspired jumpsuits in juicy hues, retro striped tees and outrageous power suits. *11am-6pm*

Avalon Vintage
see **17** P97 **D4**

One of the best-loved consignment stores in LA, Avalon is known for stocking unusual retro frocks, gowns and outfits. You'll also find an eclectic and deep collection of old vinyl records, with offerings across the genres. *noon-6pm*

Shorthand
35 P97 **B1**

Carries adorable cards and stationery, including items made by in-house letterpress printer Iron Curtain Press. There's a range of pens, pencils and other design-savvy desk essentials, as well as popular graphic-themed prints. *10am-7pm*

See p118
for eating,
drinking and
shopping
listings

Explore
Koreatown, Miracle Mile & Mid-City

Researched by
Ryan Ver Berkmoes

And the Oscar goes to... The swath of gridded streets from buzzing Koreatown in the east to the trendy zone butting up against Beverly Hills in the west claims some of LA's top cultural and retail assets. It's here that you'll find the Miracle Mile and its string of blockbuster museums, the Orthodox Jewish-meets-hipster Fairfax district, the once-trendy-now-funky Melrose Ave and the movie-studio-heavy Culver City to the south.

Sometimes called Mid-City, though that's really a specific neighborhood down by the Santa Monica Fwy, the area hosts every aspect of LA. Running through the middle is a new subway line.

Getting Around

Metro

Metro's D Line subway serves Koreatown with the Wilshire/Normandie and Wilshire/Western stations. An extension scheduled to open in 2025 will add stops on Wilshire at La Brea Ave, Fairfax Ave and La Cienega Blvd. The Wilshire/Fairfax stop promises to be LA's best transit development for visitors in decades, as it will serve several top sights like the Oscar museum and LACMA. Further extensions will serve Rodeo Dr in Beverly Hills (by 2027) and Westwood (before the 2028 Olympics). Culver City is served by the E Line.

THE BEST

ART LACMA (p112)

MOVIE MAGIC Academy Museum of Motion Pictures (p113)

ENTERTAINMENT Groundlings (p117)

NIGHT OUT Koreatown (p116)

GRAZING Original Farmers Market (p115)

Ahgassi Gopchang, Koreatown (p118)
JASON ARMOND/GETTY IMAGES

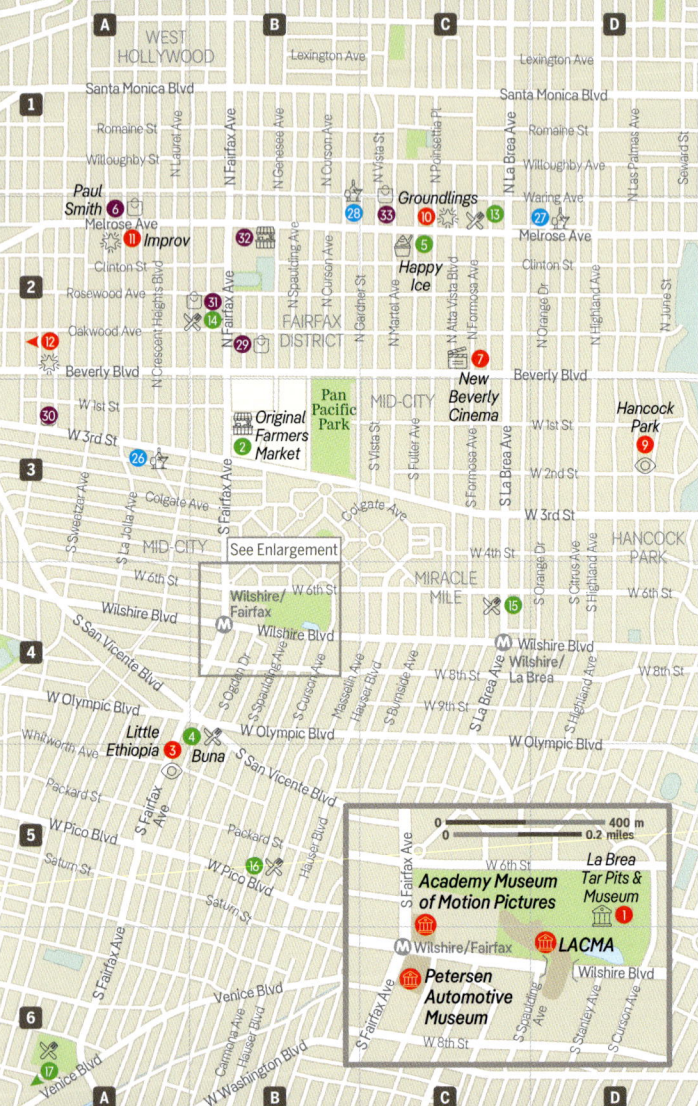

For more see

Top Experiences ★ p112
Experiences ★ p115
Eating ● p118
Drinking ● p119
Shopping ● p119

0 — 1 km
0 — 0.5 mile

Lexington Ave
Santa Monica Blvd
Hollywood Forever Cemetery
Wilcox Ave
N Cahuenga Blvd
Vine St
N Gower St
N Van Ness Ave
N Wilton Pl
N Western Ave

Melrose Ave
Clinton St
Hollywood Fwy
Maplewood Ave
Rosewood Ave
N Lucerne Blvd
N Gower St
N Bronson Ave
N Western Ave
N Normandie Ave
Rosewood Ave
Oakwood Ave

Vermont/Beverly
Beverly Blvd
The Wilshire Country Club
Beverly Blvd
N Rossmore Ave
N Arden Blvd
W 1st St
W 1st St
S Wilton Pl
S Gramercy Pl
S Manhattan Pl
W 1st St
N Harvard Blvd
N Kenmore Ave
N Berendo St
S Vermont Ave

Koreatown
8
W 2nd St
W 3rd St
W 3rd St
25
W 3rd St

S Muirfield Rd
N Rossmore Ave
S Lucerne Blvd
W 6th St
WINDSOR SQUARE
S Norton Ave
S St Andrews Pl
S Wilton Pl
S Western Ave
WILSHIRE CENTER
S Kingsley Dr
S Normandie Ave
W 4th St
W 5th St
W 5th St
W 6th St
19
24
4

Wilshire/Western
18
22
Wilshire/Vermont
Wilshire Blvd
Wilshire Blvd
S Muirfield Pl W
S Freemont Pl
Crenshaw Blvd
S Bronson Ave
Ingraham St
Wilshire/Normandie
20
Francis Ave
W 8th St
W 7th St
S Mariposa Ave
W 7th St
W 8th St
W 8th St

W Olympic Blvd
S Lucerne Ave
S Windsor Blvd
4th Ave
3rd Ave
Arlington Ave
W 9th St
Gramercy Dr
S St Andrews Pl
S Wilton Pl
S Western Ave
23
KOREATOWN
S Harvard Blvd
Irolo St
James M Wood Blvd
San Marino St
S New Hampshire Ave
S Vermont Ave

S Norton Ave
W Olympic Blvd
W Olympic Blvd
S Serrano Ave
S Kingsley Dr
S Ardmore Ave
Irolo St
21
W Olympic Blvd
Fedora St
5

W Pico Blvd
W 11th St
Country Club Dr
W Pico Blvd
W Pico Blvd
W 12th St
S Norton Ave
6th Pl
W 15th St
W 18th St
Venice Blvd
S Wilton Pl
S Gramercy Pl
S St Andrews Pl
W 18th St
Venice Blvd
Normandie Park
S Oxford Ave
S Hobart Blvd
S Kingsley Dr
W 15th St
Venice Blvd
6
Crenshaw Blvd
S Norton Ave
2nd Ave
W Washington Blvd
S Western Ave
Rosedale Cemetery
W Washington Blvd
S Vermont Ave

WALKING TOUR

Walk Culver City

Culver City is not just Hollywood's workaday sibling; today, it has more major studios than the famous neighborhood. During the 20th century, its soundstages and backlots churned out movie and TV classics. Next to Mid-City, it's one of LA's underrated pleasures: a livable, vibrant neighborhood with polished hipness and comfort.

START	END	LENGTH
Culver City Metro Station	Sony Pictures	2 miles; 2 hours

❶ Hip Start

Easily accessible by the E train, Culver City's cool factor keeps growing. Taste it at an outpost near the station, **Platform**. This buzzing outdoor development harbors niche fashion and lifestyle boutiques and trendy cafes and eateries. Stop by Loqui for fast, creative Mexican you can enjoy on the patio. Browse the industrial-chic surrounds, but then get walking as there's a lot to see.

❷ Strangely Compelling Museum

Hidden behind an inconspicuous door, the **Museum of Jurassic Technology** (*mjt.org; adult/child $15/free*) is LA's most idiosyncratic museum. It has little to do with dinosaurs or technology. Its labyrinth of curiosities would fit well in a carnival sideshow, which may be the idea. Some highlights: pre-scientific-era cures and remedies, collections found in LA trailer parks and portraits of dogs sent into space.

❸ Where 'Rosebud' Was Spoken

Many iconic movies were filmed at **Culver Studios**, such as the original *A Star is Born* (1937). Now home to Amazon Studios, its landmark Colonial Revival mansion – once the office of producer David O Selznick – is featured in the opening of *Gone With the Wind,* also filmed in and around Culver City. Other classics: *Citizen Kane* (1940) and *Planes, Trains and Automobiles* (1987).

❹ Hotel With a Past

A National Historic Landmark, the 1924 **Culver Hotel** is where 124 actors portraying Munchkins slept three-to-a-bed while filming *The Wizard of Oz*. The 1939 movie classic was shot at the nearby MGM Studios (before Sony bought it). The soundstages survive behind the tall walls, but the legendary backlot of outdoor locations is long gone. From here, Washington Blvd is lined with many shady cafes.

❺ Theater for New Works

A striking example of Streamline Moderne architecture, the 1946 **Kirk Douglas Theatre** (*centertheatregroup.org*) showcases new works by local playwrights. Across the intersection, diminutive Village Well Books attracts writers, who tap away at communal tables. Heading southwest on Culver Blvd, stop in at the Backstage Bar & Grill, a long-running dive bar popular with studio workers.

❻ Sony Pictures

Arguably the most storied of the old major studios, MGM was not in Hollywood but right here in Culver City. Today it's known as **Sony Pictures** (Amazon owns the rights to 'MGM'), and you can visit where films such as *The Wizard of Oz, Ben-Hur, Men in Black* and *Spider-Man* were shot. Countless TV series also use the studio, including *Jeopardy*. Tours depart from the Overland Gate.

The New LACMA

Soaring across Wilshire Blvd, the new **LACMA** (Los Angeles County Museum of Art) is set to open for visitors by mid-2026, displaying the stunning collection. There's millennia worth of Chinese, Japanese, pre-Columbian and ancient Greek, Roman and Egyptian sculpture, plus treasures from every continent.

MAP P108 **D6**

PLANNING TIP
Cafes are planned for admission-free public spaces on both sides of Wilshire Blvd. They should prove fine places to pause and plan visits to all four of the area museums.

Scan this QR code for full details, opening hours and tickets.

New Philosophy for a New Building

The $720-million **David Geffen Galleries** replace the museum's four aging buildings, and with it LACMA's curators are thinking of a new philosophy on how to display their huge and rich collection of art. They want to dispense with a Euro-centric and chronological narrative and instead show how works spanning mediums, cultures and time interrelate.

Unmatched Collection

Permanent collection highlights include stars like Rembrandt, Cézanne, Magritte, Mary Cassatt and Ansel Adams. Other high points: *Cold Shoulder* by Roy Lichtenstein and *Flower Day* by Diego Rivera. Two works are LA icons: *Mulholland Drive* by David Hockney and *105 Freeway* by Catherine Opie.

Outside, LACMA's Zen-like **Pavilion for Japanese Art** houses pieces ranging in origin from 3000 BCE to the present, with Chris Burden's installation *Urban Light* (a surreal selfie backdrop of vintage LA street-lamps) and Michael Heizer's *Levitated Mass,* an inspirational 340-ton boulder perched over a walkway.

Sensational Architecture

The new building is the bold vision of Swiss architect Peter Zumthor. The curvaceous, airy, cantilevered galleries straddle Wilshire Blvd. Floor-to-ceiling windows make the most of LA's natural beauty and light.

⭐ **TOP EXPERIENCE**

Academy Museum of Motion Pictures

Spoil your inner movie-lover at LA's spectacular and expansive, must-see **Academy Museum of Motion Pictures**: a cutting-edge ode to film, with thought-provoking exhibits, priceless memorabilia and movie screenings and talks delving deep into celluloid culture.

MAP P108 **C5**

Exhibitions

Start with an overview of cinema's evolution before tackling the core **Stories of Cinema** galleries. These explore the many aspects of filmmaking, as well as showcasing movie memorabilia. Items from films are all here, including a Rosebud from *Citizen Kane* and Dorothy's slippers from *The Wizard of Oz*. Scripts from blockbusters are dissected and annotated to explain the creative process. Temporary exhibitions have depth, such as Oscar-winner Bong Joon Ho (*Parasite,* 2019) detailing how he creates his films.

Special Programs

The museum's theaters host film screenings and discussions. Oscar Sundays brings out award-winning blockbusters, Silent Sundays screens neglected classics, and Branch Selects sees Academy members curating films significant to their craft. Watch for films hosted by Academy members who worked on them.

Bold Design

Designed by Italian architect Renzo Piano, the museum occupies two contrasting buildings. Entry is via the restored 1939 Streamline Moderne **Saban Building**, that once housed a May Company department store. Behind it is Piano's addition, a sphere featuring a dome with 1500 glass panels. A terrace offers sweeping views of the Hollywood Hills.

PLANNING TIP
Use the Bloomberg Connects app, which offers insights and background to greatly enhance your experience in the galleries. There's a good cafe-restaurant with outdoor seating.

Scan this QR code for a schedule of events, opening hours and to buy tickets.

★ **TOP EXPERIENCE**

Petersen Automotive Museum

The **Petersen Automotive Museum** is a treat even for those who can't tell a piston from a crankshaft. Inside the museum's body of undulating bands of stainless steel on a hot-rod-red background are four floors exploring the history, industry and artistry of motorized transportation.

MAP P108 **C6**

PLANNING TIP
This is the perfect stop if you've arrived in LA via Route 66, which passes to the north on Santa Monica Blvd and ends at the Santa Monica Pier.

Scan this QR code for details of the collection and to buy tickets.

Historic & Celebrity Cars

Vehicles are rotated through the exhibitions regularly. Start your visit on the history floor, loaded with classic and concept cars. In the Cars of Film and Television gallery, you might see the DeLorean from *Back to the Future,* the Durango 95 from *A Clockwork Orange* and always a Batmobile or two.

How Cars Are Made

The industry floor is devoted to how cars are designed and built. The displays show both the artistry and the engineering that must work in sync to get a car into production and then the many additional departments such as marketing that are required to ensure that the vehicle is an economic success. The kids' section is inspired by Disney's *Cars;* there's a custom-built Lightning McQueen. The ground floor focuses on the art of the automobile, mostly in special exhibits.

Rare & Unusual Cars

The new, extra-admission basement **Vault** displays over 300 rare cars and motorcycles. Here you won't find road-legal cars, but you'll discover rare concept cars and vehicles designed for special purposes. Many are works of art. Expect anything from Pope John Paul II's Popemobile to cars decades ahead of their time, like the 1953 Cadillac Series 62 by Ghia.

EXPERIENCES

Get Stuck on the La Brea Tar Pits
NATURAL SPECTACLE

MAP: ❶ P108 **D5**

Mammoths, saber-toothed cats and other critters roamed LA's savanna in prehistoric times. The **La Brea Tar Pits & Museum** (*tarpits.org; adult/child $18/7*) preserves a trove of skulls and bones and is one of the world's most famous fossil sites. Generations of young dino hunters have come to learn about paleontology in the museum.

The smell of asphalt permeates the air as the tar pits bubble away. A life-size diorama of a mammoth family trapped in the muck dramatizes the cruel fate of countless thousands of animals between 50,000 and 10,000 years ago. Nearby, you can observe pits where fossils are still being discovered. The entire site is now part of the Natural History Museum in Expo Park (p90).

Fun fact: *la* is Spanish for 'the' and *brea* is Spanish for 'tar,' so you're really saying 'the the Tar Tar Pits'.

Graze the Original Farmers Market
FOOD HALL

MAP: ❷ P108 **B3**

Long before LA was flooded with farmers markets, the **Original Farmers Market** (*farmersmarketla.com; hours vary*) was already operating. Once a dusty lot of produce-laden pickup trucks, the open-air 1934 landmark is now packed with casual choices for a meal or snack any time of day, from gumbo and bakery classics to tacos and pizza, sit-down or takeout. There are even a few stalls still selling produce.

Monsieur Marcel (*9am-9pm*) has a gourmet market and a seafood-centric sidewalk bistro. Fans of Michael Connelly books and Bosch will thoroughly enjoy **Du-par's** (*6am-9pm*), a legendary diner with a fine patio and a memorable banana cream pie.

Discover Little Ethiopia
NEIGHBORHOOD

Starting with Little Armenia near Los Feliz, you can run right through the alphabet of LA's great diversity of cultures. Ever changing, these enclaves are both old (Downtown's Little Tokyo) and new, like **Little Ethiopia** (MAP: ❸ P108 **A5**).

Along a block of Fairfax Ave south of Olympic Blvd, it started with one shop around 1990. As is often the case, this attracted other immigrants, and everyone's success became symbiotic. Soon it was a hub for LA's Ethiopian community, and in 2002 the city officially named the neighborhood Little Ethiopia.

Browsing the many stores, cafes and markets makes for a fine walk. The green, yellow and red of the Ethiopian flag colors storefronts. Sidewalk displays offer yams and other staples. Cafes like **Buna** (MAP: ❹ P108 **B4**; *10am-10pm*) showcase the neighborhood's vibrancy.

EDUARDO FREDERIKSEN/SHUTTERSTOCK

New Beverly Cinema

Shop Melrose Avenue & 3rd Street

SHOPPING DISTRICTS

Legendary rock-and-roll shopping strip **Melrose Avenue** is as famous for its epic people-watching as it is for its retail pleasures. The strip between N Poinsettia Pl and N Fairfax Ave gets a lot of the buzz thanks to the boutiques stuck together like block-long hedgerows. Most of its gear is rather low-end, so amuse yourself browsing, then get sweet at **Happy Ice** (MAP: **5** P108 **C2**; *noon-9pm*). If you're after hipper, higher-end stuff, explore the long stretch of Melrose between N Crescent Heights Blvd and Santa Monica Blvd. Stop for selfie joy at the **Paul Smith** (MAP: **6** P108 **A2**) clothing store's Barbie-pink wall. Or hit **3rd Street** in the same area, which is the current place to find attitude outpacing style and cars idling in traffic with sticker prices beyond the means of the 99%.

Catch Great Films at New Beverly Cinema

CLASSIC FILM THEATER

MAP: **7** P108 **C2**

Quentin Tarantino owns the vintage 1920s **New Beverly Cinema** (*thenewbev.com; pictured above*), which screens classic, cult, current and art films. All are projected in 35mm, with many of the restored prints from the owner's collection. He also owns the Vista Theater (p79) in Los Feliz. Some programs are double features, and many include classic Bugs Bunny cartoons. The crowd is heavy with industry types, who stand up front before the lights go down discussing projects and deals.

Party in Nonstop Koreatown

NEIGHBORHOOD

MAP: **8** P108 **G3**

Koreatown is as close as LA gets to being the 'city that never sleeps.' Sprawling and vibrant, it's a platter of sizzling barbecue joints, buzzing malls and karaoke bars, all splashed with a dash of glorious Moderne architecture from the area's gilded past when it was a bastion of Golden Age Hollywood. The area is roughly bounded by Beverly and Olympic Blvds north and south, plus Western Ave on the west. The eastern side abuts MacArthur Park, the one that 'melts in the dark' in the eponymous Jimmy Webb song made famous by Donna Summer. Wilshire Blvd is the main artery, as well as W 6th St, S Vermont Ave and W 8th St.

Koreatown has a vast number of eateries. Enjoy *soju-* (rice alcohol) or *makgeolli-* (rice wine) fueled swilling at a sweaty drinking den or in a *noraebang* (private karaoke room) hangout.

Just to keep things geographically off-kilter, there's a cluster of superb Oaxacan restaurants.

Laugh at Live Comedy
COMEDY SHOWS

Three of the top venues for live comedy are found in Mid-City. Most famous is **Groundlings** (MAP: **10** P108 **C2**; *groundlings.com*), where the Improv alums include Lisa Kudrow, Will Ferrell, Maya Rudolph and Melissa McCarthy. On Thursday the main company, alumni and surprise guests riff together.

The Improv (MAP: **11** P108 **A2**; *improv.com*) is another venue with a pedigree. It's been the launch pad for countless stand-up comics from Richard Pryor to Jerry Seinfeld, Ellen DeGeneres and Dave Chapelle. It mixes its namesake style of comedy with headliners.

The comedy takes many forms at **Largo at the Coronet** (MAP: **12** P108 **A2**; *largo-la.com*), an incubator of high-minded pop culture and part of the Coronet Theatre complex. It features edgy comedy as well as nourishing night music.

HANCOCK PARK
MAP: **9** P108 **D3**

Century-old mansions flank the tree-lined streets of **Hancock Park**, a genteel neighborhood roughly bounded by Highland, Rossmore and Melrose Aves and Wilshire Blvd. In the 1920s, LA's leading families, including the Dohenys and Chandlers, hired famous architects to build their cribs, and numerous celebrities have lived here amid the curving lawns. It remains popular with investment bankers, high-end lawyers and entertainment-industry types.

As you stroll or drive this lovely neighborhood, it's hard to believe the ugly aspects of its history. It was long a whites-only area, and when Nat King Cole bought a house here in 1948, his dog was poisoned.

LISTINGS

Best Places for...

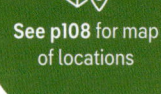

See p108 for map of locations

$** Budget   **$$** Midrange   **$$$ Top End

Eating

Classic Casual Bites

Pink's Hot Dogs $
 C2

Famous doggeria (since 1939) that features glacially moving lines. But the reason for coming is worth it: garlicky all-beef frankfurters drenched in chili. *9:30am-midnight*

Canter's $
14 **B2**

This deli isn't closed, despite its veteran appearance. Beloved for legendary pastrami and other standards, which are all good. Great bakery items, comfy booths, knowledgeable servers. Parking. *6am-11:30pm*

Top Tables

République $$
15 **C4**

Sports several fetching hats: artisan bakery, light-filled cafe and buzzing bistro, all near the rarified air of Hancock Park. The open kitchen pumps out daily-changing French-accented dishes and unmissable desserts. *8am-2pm & 5:30-10pm*

My 2 Cents LA $$$
 B5

The acclaimed restaurant of TV chef Alisa Reynolds has a loyal following for her wonderful Southern fusion fare. A haven for A-listers including former president Barack Obama. Reserve ahead. *11:30am-9:30pm Thu-Sun*

Dear John's $$$
17 **A6**

Revitalized in 2019, this comforting Culver City steakhouse dates to the Sinatra era. Everything is on point from the moment you sit in the deeply padded booth. The tater tots are even dotted with caviar. *5:30-9:30pm Tue-Sat*

Koreatown Eats

Ahgassi Gopchang $$
 G4

Popular with the young and families. Get to this K-town cafe early to avoid long lines. Pics of happy luminaries enjoying the bulgogi cover the walls. *11:30am-midnight*

Danbi $$$
19 **H4**

In historic Chapman Plaza you'll find gracious Korean fusion fine dining, thoughtfully prepared and artfully served. The menu changes regularly; servers walk you through esoteric options. *6-10pm Wed-Sun*

Langer's Deli $$$
20 **H4**

By MacArthur Park, an old-school sit-down deli famous for Sandwich 19 (peppery pastrami, Swiss cheese and coleslaw on double-baked rye). Busy at lunch, but there are always free seats at the counter. Parking. *8am-4pm Mon-Sat*

Guelaguetza Restaurant $$
21 **G5**

Renowned for its award-winning, rich mole, this restaurant anchors a vibrant Oaxacan community and has been a notable feature of Koreatown since the 1990s. There are more good choices nearby. *9am-9pm*

Drinking

Koreatown Imbibing

Normandie Club

 G4

This dimly lit bar is cool yet approachable. The talented staff whip up creative cocktails for imbibers, lovers and first dates. Get the potent old-fashioned made with a wink and a nod. *6pm-2am*

Rosen Karaoke

23 **G5**

A popular spot for great service and private rooms in varying sizes. Sing, snack and drink yourself happy. There's a good tunes selection for you to mangle. *7pm-2am*

Dan Sung Sa

24 **H4**

In a tatty strip mall, this minimalist storefront mimics a Seoul street bar with tight wooden booths, potent *soju* cocktails and ribald revelry. *4pm-2am*

Lock & Key

25 **H3**

Look for the neon sign with a key on it and enter. Classy, with candles on tables and a cool dance patio. Note that the dress code eschews most bro-wear. *7pm-2am*

Miracle Mile & Fairfax Bars

El Carmen

26 **A3**

Loud, dimly lit and full of bull heads and *lucha libre* (Mexican wrestling) memorabilia. This tequila tavern pulls an industry-heavy crowd. *5pm-2am*

Stir Crazy

27 **D2**

A neighborhood favorite with tables out front, with rare California wines by the glass. Daily specials. Small plates add to the enjoyment. *5-11pm Mon-Fri*

Be Bright Coffee

see **10** **C2**

Popular cafe roasting its own beans, used by restaurants across LA. Expertly brewed coffee. Plenty of tea options. *8am-4pm*

Snake Pit

28 **B2**

A long-running dive bar on Melrose. Good drink prices and a big selection of whiskey. Popular burgers. *3am-midnight*

Shopping

Fairfax Picks

Golf Wang

29 **B2**

Rapper Tyler, the Creator, known for his alterna-

tive hip-hop, owns this clothing store that reflects his vision of cool. One of many on this strip. *11am-7pm*

Polkadots & Moonbeams

30 **A3**

Whimsical yet exceptional vintage womenswear shop stocked with affordable designer dresses, shades, scarves and hats. *11am-5pm*

Ripndip

31 **B2**

Streetwear, skatewear and skateboards. The logo will look familiar to tire buyers, and the same wit runs through all the gear. *11am-7pm*

Melrose Trading Post

32 **B2**

Every Sunday more than 250 vendors sell threads, jewelry, housewares, crafts and other offbeat items in the Fairfax High parking lot. Trends start here. *10am-5pm Sun*

Posers Hollywood

33 **C2**

Embodies the old Melrose Ave today. Dr Martens, Fred Perry and other punkish wear. Tourists pose with their new duds on out front. *noon-6pm*

See p128
for eating,
drinking and
shopping
listings

Explore
West Hollywood & Beverly Hills

Researched by
Ryan Ver Berkmoes

Famous worldwide, the 90210 zip code is a status symbol for wealthy A-list celebrities, luxe hotels and top-of-the-line shopping. Today, visitors flock to Beverly Hills to get a taste of the fantasy and to take in the opulent real estate and swaying palm trees.

Next door, but a world apart, West Hollywood (aka WeHo) is distinctly, proudly independent. With some of LA's finest bars, renowned live music, hedonistic nightlife and the famous (even if faded) Sunset Strip, WeHo has enough draw to rival a famous zip code. More importantly, it's a thriving LGBTQ+ community. It parties in June for Pride and in October for Halloween.

Getting Around

 Metro

When the Metro Rail Line D Wilshire/Rodeo station opens – possibly in 2026 – it will revolutionize access to Beverly Hills. Until then, Metro Bus Line 4 runs frequently along Santa Monica Blvd in West Hollywood and Beverly Hills. Metro Bus Line 2 connects Sunset Blvd in West Hollywood to Westwood, Hollywood, Silver Lake, Echo Park and Downtown LA.

 Car

Parking in WeHo and Beverly Hills is never easy and usually expensive. Both areas are walkable, although WeHo is hilly at the edges.

THE BEST

PLACE TO PARTY
WeHo (p126)

CONSPICUOUS CONSUMPTION
Beverly Hills (p124)

TOURS
Bikes & Hikes LA (p126)

THOUGHTFUL MUSEUM
Museum of Tolerance (p126)

HOLLYWOOD DREAM
Polo Lounge (p129)

Rodeo Drive, Beverly Hills (p124)
MICHAEL GORDON/SHUTTERSTOCK

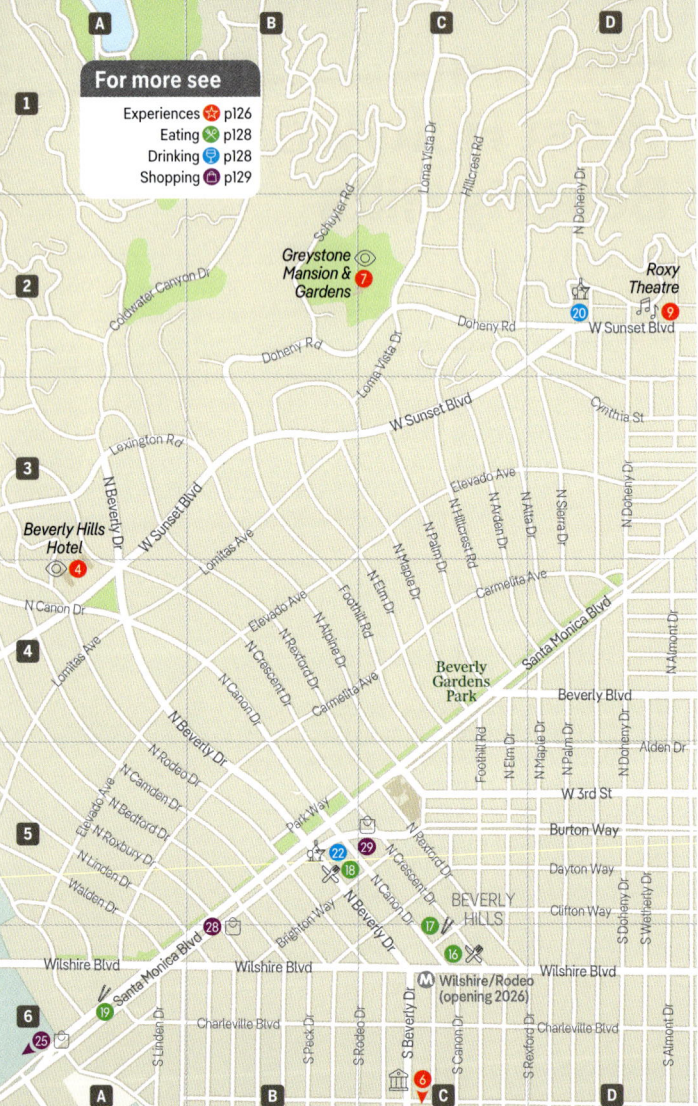

For more see

Experiences ⭐ p126
Eating ✖ p128
Drinking 🍷 p128
Shopping 🛍 p129

Greystone Mansion & Gardens ⑦

Roxy Theatre
⑳ ⑨ W Sunset Blvd

Beverly Hills Hotel ④

Beverly Gardens Park

BEVERLY HILLS

Wilshire/Rodeo
(opening 2026)

E   F   G   H

Hollywood Blvd

Laurel
Canyon
Blvd

Laugh
Factory
11

W Sunset Blvd

1

Comedy
Store
10

William S Hart
Park
14

Fountain Ave

N Crescent Heights Blvd

Fountain Ave

WEST
HOLLYWOOD

SUNSET
STRIP

W Sunset Blvd

N La Cienega Blvd

N Flores St

N Sweetzer Ave

Norton Ave

2

Whisky-
a-Go-Go
8

Holloway Dr

Olive Dr
13

26

24 23

WEST
HOLLYWOOD

Santa Monica Blvd

Bikes &
Hikes LA
5

Santa Monica Blvd
3
Hamburger
Mary's

Romaine St

N Laurel Ave

N Edinburgh Ave

N Hayworth Ave

N Fairfax Ave

3

Plann Ave

Santa Monica Blvd

West Knoll Dr

N La Cienega Blvd

N Kings Rd

N Sweetzer Ave

Willoughby   St

Waring   Ave

Micky's
WeHo
2

Huntley Dr

Melrose Ave

Abbey
1

21

BEVERLY
CENTER
DISTRICT

Clinton St

S Edinburgh Ave

N Fairfax Ave

Melrose Ave
15

Huntley Dr

N San Vicente Blvd

Rosewood Ave

N Genesee Ave

4

N Robertson Blvd

N La Cienega Blvd

Oakwood Ave

N Crescent Heights Blvd

27

Beverly Blvd

Beverly Blvd

Alden Dr

W 1st St

The
Grove

W 3rd St

Burton Way

W 3rd St

5

Colgate Ave

S Swall Dr

N Robertson Blvd

S Hamel Dr

S Sherbourne Dr

S Carling St

S San Vicente Blvd

N La Cienega Blvd

S Orlando Ave

S Sweetzer Ave

Colgate Ave

S La Jolla Ave

S Crescent Heights Blvd

S Fairfax Ave

Wilshire Blvd

6

Charleville Blvd

N

0   1 km
0   0.5 miles

E   F   G   H

Walk Beverly Hills

Stroll Rodeo Dr and discover notable art and iconic architecture and get your picture taken – yep, you're in Beverly Hills! The gilded residents hide in neighborhoods like cloistered Bel Air with its 16ft hedges and walls. But in the commercial heart of the city you can at least share in the fantasy on a short walk.

START	END	LENGTH
Rodeo Dr & Wilshire Blvd	Beverly Gardens Park	0.75 miles; 2 hours

1 Rodeo Drive's Start

From the corner of **Rodeo Drive** and Wilshire Blvd, begin your walk up the vaunted three-block ribbon of consumption that features every major luxury brand on the planet. Many change their facades as often as more humble stores change their window displays. Rodeo Dr's first boutique opened in 1961. Before that it was simple residential homes, and in the 1880s the entire area was lima bean farms.

2 Famous Shopping

Architecturally, nothing is especially noteworthy – even the Frank Lloyd Wright–designed **Anderton Court Shops** at No 328 are ho-hum. Typical Frank Lloyd Wright anecdote: he only blew through his strict budget by a factor of 2. Rather, a successful day here is measured by the number of glossy brand-name shopping bags you can carry. Celebrities all go to private boutiques, so don't expect to see any.

3 Wild Art

When you reach inner Santa Monica Blvd, turn right for one block. **Mr Brainwash Art Museum** (*mrbrainwashartmuseum.com; adult/child $20/free)* is the namesake project of the French-born Banksy protégé who's based in LA. It's crammed with his whimsical kitsch-meets-fine-art: the Hollywood Sign pops up in a Van Gogh, a cat appears in a Keith Haring, Warhol's here and there, you get the idea...

4 Sci-Fi Gas

Two streets east, the **Union 76 Gas Station** is a famous example of Googie architecture and is spectacular at night. The swooping, back-to-the-future canopy is fit for a 1950s sci-fi movie. Googie is a mid-century, SoCal style reflecting the era's burgeoning space-age and car culture. The architect, Gin D Wong, also designed the renowned Theme Building in the middle of LAX airport.

5 Proclaiming Wealth

Swing around to Crescent Dr and the **Beverly Hills Civic Center**, a grand 1932 Spanish Revival edifice. Built right as the Depression was setting in across the US and the world, it was the city's proclamation that the movie industry wouldn't be bothered by a mere global economic collapse. The blue, green and gold tiled dome proclaims the local wealth for miles around.

6 Beverly Hills' Park

Now, cross into **Beverly Gardens Park**. Stretching nearly 2 miles, this green swath dating to 1911 is the manicured, statue-dotted, flower-filled border to commercial Beverly Hills. Highlights in the park include the rose and cactus gardens, the lily pond and the century-old Moreton Bay fig. The finish point of the walk, the 40ft-long **'Beverly Hills' sign**, might as well spell s-e-l-f-i-e.

EXPERIENCES

Partying in West Hollywood   NEIGHBORHOOD

Santa Monica Blvd is WeHo's main drag, and barhopping its length is one of the LA region's great joys. The LGBTQ+-centric bars and clubs heave through the weekends, with Sunday brunch a must, while weeknights are busy too.

One of the most iconic gay nightclubs on the West Coast today, is the **Abbey** (MAP: ❶ P122 **E3**; *11am-2am*), which serves the community as much as a cultural center as a bar and nightclub. Match your mood to the space: thumping dance floor, outdoor patios, Goth lounge or chill space.

The boulevard abounds with choices like the iconic **Micky's WeHo** (MAP: ❷ P122 **E3**; *noon-2am*), with long-running drag shows and great DJ sets. **Hamburger Mary's** (MAP: ❸ P122 **G2**; *11am-10pm*) is the Sunday afternoon brunch go-to.

Live the Life in Beverly Hills   NEIGHBORHOOD

With it's name a shorthand for ostentatious wealth and celebrity, Beverly Hills is as much a state of mind as a place. Ultimately, however, it's a rich, tidy place without a plethora of must-see sights; rather, you go to soak up the vibe, nibble a bit of the fantasy and think about what life would be like if that was your Lamborghini parked on Rodeo Dr.

On a short walk (p124), you can take in the heart of the neighborhood.

Drop by the **Beverly Hills Hotel** (MAP: ❹ P122 **A4**), the famed 'pink palace' that's never lost its sheen of glamour and where the **Polo Lounge** (p129) or the **Cabana Cafe** remain the ultimate Beverly Hills experience. Have a martini and mourn the coming of cell phones, which ended the tradition of fading celebs calling the hotel and having themselves paged to remind producers of their existence.

Tour LA the Active Way   CYCLING AND HIKING TOURS

MAP: ❺ P122 **F3**

See Hollywood, Beverly Hills and greater LA on highly recommended tours with **Bikes & Hikes LA** (*bikesandhikesla.com*). Its signature ride is the 32-mile 'LA in a Day,' which takes in celebrity homes, swank shopping streets, inspiring architecture and the Pacific. Other options include shorter tours and e-bikes. Hiking tours include a 1½-hour jaunt to the Hollywood Sign.

Experience the Museum of Tolerance   HUMAN RIGHTS MUSEUM

MAP: ❻ P122 **C6**

Learning the hard lessons of humanity's past so they aren't repeated is at the core of the **Museum of Tolerance** *(museumoftolerance.com; adult/ child $18/13.50)*. The human cost of intolerance is relentlessly detailed on each floor. Among the museum's many fascinating artifacts are original diary entries written by Anne Frank as well as the first record of Hitler's anti-Semitic beliefs.

Visitors, including many school groups, are given the persona of a child who died in the **Holocaust** and then follow an effective and gripping exhibit about the events that shows the influence of major donor Steven Spielberg. In the basement, the **Social Lab** is an immersive and interactive exploration of how we are driven apart through prejudice and bigotry. It's effective and timely.

Tour Greystone Mansion & Gardens
HISTORIC MANSION

MAP: **7** P122 **C2**

Looking just like you'd expect a Beverly Hills mansion to look, the free **Greystone Mansion & Gardens** has featured in countless movies and TV shows *(The Big Lebowski, There Will Be Blood)*. This 1927 Tudor Revival pile was a gift from oil tycoon Edward Doheny to his son Ned. In 1929, the oil heir and his male secretary were both found dead in an alleged murder-suicide – a notorious mystery that has been debated endlessly ever since.

The **elegant grounds**, with their perfectly coiffed lawns,

BEST LIVE MUSIC & COMEDY

Whisky-a-Go-Go

MAP: **8** P122 **E2**

The Whisky trades on its legendary status when the Doors were the house band and go-go dancing was invented here back in the '60s. *whiskyagogo.com*

Roxy Theatre

MAP: **9** P122 **D2**

A Sunset Strip fixture since 1973, this small venue puts you close to the bands. The lineup varies, with some big-name surprises. *theroxy.com*

Comedy Store

MAP: **10** P122 **F2**

The club with credibility. Richard Pryor, George Carlin, Eddie Murphy, Robin Williams and David Letterman were nurtured here, and the tradition continues. *thecomedystore.com*

Laugh Factory

MAP: **11** P122 **G1**

The Marx Brothers used to keep offices at this long-standing club. Gets big names trying out new sets, up-and-comers and surprise celebs. *laughfactory.com*

Italian Renaissance fountains and 166ft walkway with enormous cypress trees, offer commanding views of LA.

LISTINGS

Best Places for...

$ Budget $$ Midrange $$$ Top End

See p122 for map of locations

Eating

In West Hollywood

Tail O' the Pup $
 F3

Look for the big weenie in a bun. Hot dogs served in myriad ways (the 'jalapeño pup' will perk you right up); also burgers, corndogs, fries and even grilled cheese. Shady tables, too. *noon-10pm*

Barney's Beanery $$
13 **F2**

Burger and beer bar has fronted Santa Monica Blvd since it was better known as Route 66 and overheated Studebakers steamed out front. Has a loyal following. *11am-2am*

Tower Bar $$$
14 **F2**

Old-school Hollywood luxury packaged in an indoor-outdoor setting at the swank Sunset Tower Hotel. Vaunted martinis and high-end burgers match the sublime views.

Note the warnings to their upscale guests about proper behavior. *7am-10pm*

Catch LA $$$
15 **E4**

You may find paparazzi stalking celebrity guests, but such distractions are forgotten once you saunter into this 3rd-floor rooftop restaurant-bar. Graze on East–West, surf-centric share plates. Optional vegan menu. *6-10pm*

In Beverly Hills

Spago $$$
16 **C6**

Wolfgang Puck still turns up to work at his foundational restaurant, where California flavors are celebrated with the changing seasons. The smoked-salmon pizza is an icon. *5:30-9:30pm*

Sugarfish $$$
17 **C6**

Quality sushi in a small space that's always packed with talent agents and residents. The 20-course tasting menu is pure pleasure and a wonderful adventure

in Japanese cuisine. *11:30am-10pm*

Nate'n Al's $$
18 **B5**

Get a bowl of piping-hot matzo-ball soup and a Brentwood sandwich at this institution, shining after a refresh driven by Hollywood moguls. The most appealing sidewalk tables are close to Rodeo Dr. *8am-9pm*

Joss Cuisine $$
19 **A6**

Warm, intimate restaurant serving superlative Chinese cuisine at non-celebrity prices. Premium produce drives everything from the flawless dim sum and ginger fish broth to crispy mustard prawns and fine Peking duck. *5-10pm*

Drinking

In West Hollywood

Bar Next Door
20 **D2**

Enticing cocktail bar with a solid backlist of

creations going back more than a century. Has rare libations that get mixed in fabulous ways. Many come just for the cheery, mellow vibe. *5pm-2am*

EP & LP

 21 **F3**

Sip excellent cocktails at one of LA's largest and most popular rooftop bars. Pick a table under a palm tree and savor the views. On many nights, the Melrose Rooftop Theatre (*melroserooftoptheatre. com*) screens films. *4pm-2am*

In Beverly Hills

Polo Lounge

see **4** **A4**

Dress up and swill martinis in the Beverly Hills Hotel's legendary bar. Movies still matter here, and studio titans really do hammer out deals at the tables, while top celebs huddle with agents. *7am-1:30am*

Wally's Beverly Hills

 22 **B5**

Great wine bar with outdoor seating and a huge list of wine, mezcal and champagne. Also cheese platters and elegant bites. *10am-12:30am*

Shopping

In West Hollywood

Book Soup

23 **E2**

Great indie bookstore with thoughtful staff recs. The source for eclectic, edgy and LA-based fiction amid 60,000 titles. Good entertainment-biz section. Author events feature big names. *9am-9pm*

Mystery Pier Books

24 **E2**

Jewel box of a shop stocking signed shooting scripts from blockbusters and rare 1st editions of books. Amid the treasures is a curated selection of mystery and detective fiction. Ask for LA-based recommendations – there are many! *11am-6pm*

Giant Robot

25 **A6**

West of Beverly Hills, fans of anime will find their happy place rifling through the T-shirts, action figures, stuffed creatures, books and more at this ode to the weird, ugly and cute. *noon-6pm*

Pleasure Chest

26 **H2**

The perfect boutique to accessorize your soiree

in WeHo. Most tastes and desires are catered for in this adult novelty store. *10am-9pm*

Curve

27 **E4**

Funky fashion boutique that isn't as stiff as some of the other players on Robertson. Denim, jewelry and a range of trenches, spiked heels, sexy minis, leather vests and baby-doll dresses. *11am-6pm*

In Beverly Hills

Cheese Store

28 **B6**

After featuring in one of the final episodes of *Curb Your Enthusiasm,* the shop had to set up a section for 'Larry David's cheese.' With a superb selection of prepared foods, this is the place to get outfitted for a picnic in Beverly Gardens Park. *10am-5pm*

Edelweiss Chocolates

29 **C5**

Old-school shop; that woman buying a box of chocolates looks like the one who played the mother on the old sit-com you watched when you were home sick from school. Delicious confections eschew trends for solid flavors done well. *10am-6pm*

⭐ **WORTH A TRIP**

Getty Center

Straddling a hilltop in the Santa Monica Mountains, the unmissable Getty Center offers a feast of art, design and botanical beauty. Ponder the myths and landscapes of great European artists, gaze out over the Southland and kick back in a verdant wonderland with world-famous sculptures.

GETTING THERE
The Getty is best reached by car. While admission is free, you must book a timed-entry reservation in advance, which includes a **reserved parking space** (*$25, after 3pm $15*).

Scan this QR code for opening hours and to book an entrance time.

Collections

The Getty's collections focus on European art, with a concentration on works from the 19th and 20th centuries. There are myriad genuine treasures here.

In the east pavilion, seek out Gentileschi's *Danaë and the Shower of Gold* and Rembrandt's *Abduction of Europa,* and his self-portrait *Rembrandt Laughing*. In the west pavilion, look for Van Gogh's *Irises,* Monet's *Wheatstacks, Snow Effect, Morning,* Manet's *Jeanne (Spring)* and Turner's *Modern Rome – Campo Vaccino*. The north pavilion includes Titian's *Venus and Adonis*. The south pavilion's terrace is home to Marino Marini's excitable bronze *Angel of the Citadel*. The grounds are studded with prized sculptures, including three works by Henry Moore.

Architecture & Gardens

As famous for its form as for its art, the Getty Center (pictured right) originated from the drawing board of Pritzker Prize-winning architect Richard Meier. Completed in 1997 at a cost of $1.3 billion, the complex is clad in 16,000 tons of cleft-cut travertine sourced from the same Italian quarry used to construct Rome's ancient Colosseum. Look closely and you'll spot fossilised shells, fish and foliage.

Even getting up to the 110-acre campus aboard the driverless tram is fun. From the sprawling arrival plaza, a natural flow of walkways, stairs, fountains

WALTER CICCHETTI/SHUTTERSTOCK

and courtyards encourages a leisurely wander between galleries, gardens and outdoor cafes. Don't miss the lovely **Cactus Garden** on the remote South Promontory for breathtaking city views.

Events & Visiting Practicalities

Free tours are offered throughout the day. There is also a variety of mostly free events such as talks, symposia and curated film screenings. Some require reservations, though standby tickets are often available. Get the essential **GettyGuide** app, which has maps (needed!) and details about the artworks. **Free audio guides** are available in the lobby (bring a photo ID).

On Saturday evenings from May to September, the center hosts **Off the 405**, a popular series of free perfomances featuring top progressive pop and world-music acts in the Getty courtyard. Book ahead.

TOP TIP
Visit early morning or after 3pm to avoid crowds. Sunsets create a remarkable alchemy of light and shadow; find a special place on the grounds for viewing.

See p140
for eating,
drinking and
shopping
listings

Explore
Santa Monica

Researched by
Ryan Ver Berkmoes

Santa Monica is LA's little sister, its smaller, beachier twin, with glass towers abutting the famous pier and amusement park. Surrounded by the city on three sides and the Pacific on the fourth, here surfers bob in the waves, laid-back dudes sip hazy brews next to martini-swilling Hollywood producers, and celebrity chefs rub elbows with on-point soccer moms at bountiful farmers markets.

The E Rail means you can avoid the Santa Monica Fwy and arrive right at the sand, ready for all the coastal pleasures. Elsewhere, appealing commercial strips on Montana Ave and Main St are where relaxed nightlife is the norm.

Getting Around

 Metro

Santa Monica is well served by the Metro Rail E Line, which goes directly downtown (50 minutes) and provides easy links to LAX and beyond. Metro Bus 4 follows Santa Monica Blvd through Beverly Hills and Hollywood to DTLA. Santa Monica's municipal Big Blue Bus travels around town and to the LAX Transit Center.

 Car

Beachside parking fees add up quickly. For Santa Monica, take the train. Santa Monica is also enjoyably walkable, especially on the bluff overlooking the beaches, which flow right into Venice.

THE BEST

FAMILY DAY OUT
Santa Monica Pier (p138)
————————
BEACH PATH Marvin
Braude Bike Trail (p139)
————————
ARTS CENTER
Bergamot Station
Arts Center (p139)
————————
SANDWICH
Bay Cities Italian Deli
& Bakery (p140)
————————
DINNER WITH A VIEW
Élephante (p140)

Santa Monica Pier (p138)

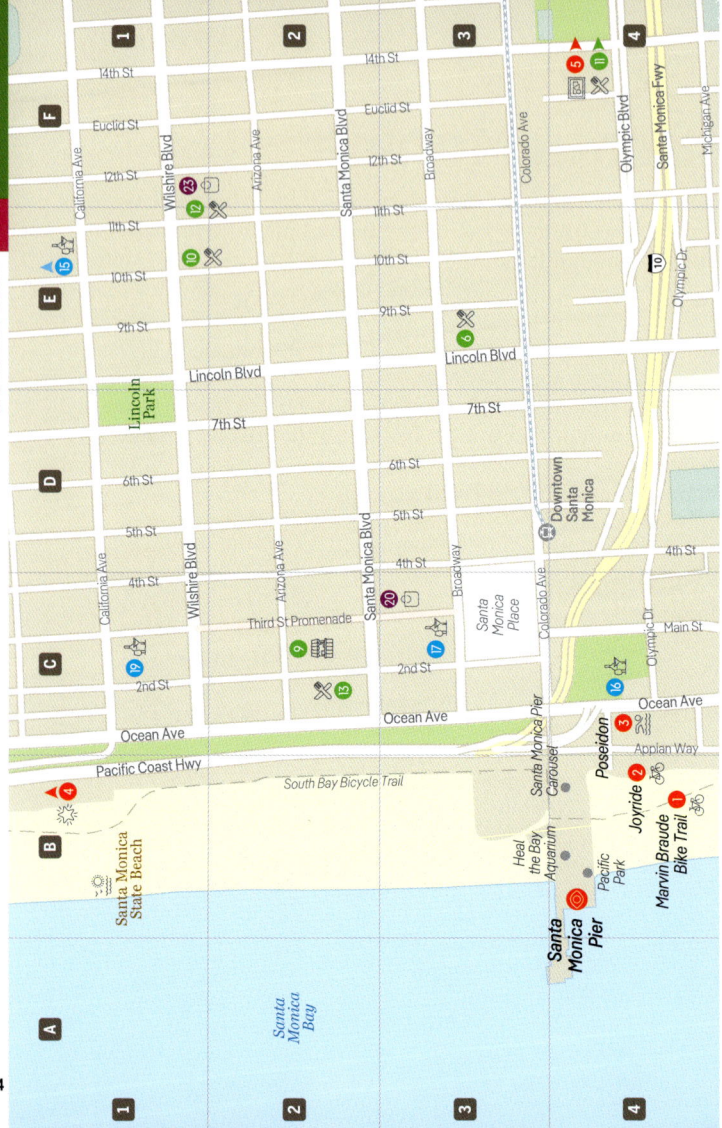

1
2
3
4

14th St

14th St

5

11

Olympic Blvd

Santa Monica Fwy

Michigan Ave

F

Euclid Ave

Euclid Ave

California Ave

Wilshire Blvd

12th St

23

12th St

Arizona Ave

Santa Monica Blvd

Broadway

Colorado Ave

Olympic Blvd

11th St

12

11th St

E

15

10

10th St

10th St

10

Olympic Dr

9th St

9th St

Lincoln Blvd

6

Lincoln Blvd

7th St

7th St

Lincoln Park

Lincoln Blvd

D

6th St

6th St

4th St

Wilshire Blvd

5th St

5th St

Downtown Santa Monica

California Ave

4th St

Arizona Ave

Santa Monica Blvd

4th St

Broadway

Colorado Ave

Santa Monica Place

Main St

Olympic Dr

C

19

Third St Promenade

9

20

17

Santa Monica Pier Carousel

16

2nd St

13

2nd St

Ocean Ave

Ocean Ave

Poseidon

3

4

Ocean Ave

Pacific Coast Hwy

South Bay Bicycle Trail

Santa Monica Pier

Applan Way

Joyride

2

1

Heal the Bay Aquarium

Pacific Park

Marvin Braude Bike Trail

B

Santa Monica State Beach

Santa Monica Pier

A

Santa Monica Bay

1
2
3
4

For more see

⭐ Top Experiences p138
✪ Experiences p139
🍴 Eating p140
🍷 Drinking p140
🛍 Shopping p141

500 m
0.25 miles

14th St
Euclid St
12th St
11th St
10th St
9th St
Lincoln Blvd
4th St
Ocean Ave
Appian Way

Pico Blvd
Euclid St
Pacific St
Pearl St
Cedar St
Pine St
7th St
Bay St
10th St

Lincoln Blvd
7th St

Santa Monica High School

6th St
5th St
4th St
3rd St

Hollister Ave
5th St
Ocean Park Blvd
Hill St
4th St
Ashland Ave

Pico Blvd
Bay St
Main St
Main St
Nelson Way
Barnard Way
Bay St

2nd St
Nelson Way
Main St
Barnard Way

South Bay Bicycle Trail

Santa Monica State Beach

Santa Monica Bay

WALKING TOUR

Stroll Santa Monica's Beach

Santa Monica is a city defined by its beach. The long ribbon of sand is its pleasurable border with the Pacific and the daily vermilion sunsets. You can walk the length of the beach and appreciate many of Santa Monica's iconic attractions like the pier, then turn inland to Main St for background and refreshments.

START	END	LENGTH
Will Rogers State Beach	California Heritage Museum	3 miles; 3 hours

① Start on the Sand

Begin at the popular south volleyball courts on **Will Rogers State Beach**. Nearly 2 miles long, this sandy beach is the answer to the oft-asked question: 'Where was *Baywatch* shot?' Although the show implied that David Hasselhoff, Pamela Anderson and the rest saved swimmers from sharks and serial killers in Santa Monica, most exterior scenes were shot on the production-friendly sands here. Follow the Ocean Front Walk southeast.

② The Original Malibu

This part of the beach was known as the Gold Coast in the 1920s and '30s, when it was an early Malibu. Cary Grant lived at 1039 Palisades Beach Rd with his close friend Randolph Scott. Now part of the Annenberg Community Beach House (p139), the **Davies Guest House** *(tours noon-2pm Fri-Mon)* has a formal elegance you'd never find in a beach house today.

③ Santa Monica's Beach

The sand morphs into **Santa Monica State Beach**, where there are nearly endless ways to enjoy this 3.5-mile stretch that runs seamlessly into Venice Beach (p150) in the south. Should you want to ride rather than walk, Joyride (p139) has rental outlets at the start of this walk or just south of the pier. Or pause for a plunge in the surf.

④ Under the Famous Pier

Look up along the underside of the **Santa Monica Pier** (p138), a landmark with a history as twisted as some of the timber braces. It's really two piers: the wide 1916 pleasure pier that doesn't extend far over the surf, and the much longer and narrower 1909 pier that carried the city's sewer pipes out into the ocean (now it carries tourists).

⑤ Weighty Attraction

South of the pier, look for the ropes, parallel bars and swings of the **Original Muscle Beach**, where the Southern California exercise craze began in the 1930s and '40s. While it's more landmark than active gym and doesn't attract gawkers like Muscle Beach (p150) south in Venice, it's free and open to the public, has updated equipment and draws a fresh generation of fitness buffs.

⑥ On to Main Street

Here's your chance to head inland from the sand. The **California Heritage Museum** *(californiaheritagemuseum.org; adult/child $10/free)* is housed in one of Santa Monica's few surviving grand Victorian mansions (1894). Amid exhibits on Santa Monica's heritage are lively displays covering its foundational roles in skateboarding and in popularizing surfing. Outside are cafes and more.

⭐ **TOP EXPERIENCE**

Santa Monica Pier

No visit to LA is complete without a stroll on historic **Santa Monica Pier**, which features on about every LA tourist ad. Stretching almost a quarter-mile over the Pacific, it's the end point of iconic Route 66, which begins 2400 miles east in Chicago.

MAP P134 **B4**

PLANNING TIP
One of LA's best deals, Pacific Park regularly runs a special where buying unlimited day passes *(adult/ child $50/30)* for two days gets the rest of the year included for free.

Scan this QR code for details on attractions and opening hours.

Pacific Park

Dating to 1908, the pier is the city's most compelling landmark. Every angle is dominated by the **Pacific Park** *(pacpark.com; rides from $8)* and its family-friendly arcades, carnival games, soaring **Ferris wheel** and tame **roller coaster** (the West Coaster!). There are 12 rides total, with most designed to delight younger sensibilities.

Other Attractions

A National Historic Landmark at the beginning of the pier, **Santa Monica Pier Carousel** is housed in the 1916 Hippodrome building. The merry-go-round appeared in *The Sting* (1973) and has 44 horses plus one rabbit and one goat. Music evokes an old calliope, and the old-time soda fountain continues to delight adults and kids. The pier is most photogenic when framed by California sunsets. At night it comes alive with a neon spectacle on the rides. Watch for free concerts and outdoor movies in summer.

Aquarium

Under the Santa Monica Pier, just below the carousel, is the small **Heal the Bay Aquarium** *(healthebay .org/aquarium; adult/child $12/5),* sponsored by environmental group Heal the Bay. Kid-friendly touch tanks crawl with crabs and crustaceans from local waters. Get close to an eel in the reef area and browse an exhibit on the kelp forests growing just offshore.

EXPERIENCES

Cycle the Beaches
BIKE TRAIL

Tour LA's world-famous beaches by riding the 22-mile **Marvin Braude Bike Trail** (MAP: **1** P134 **B4**). The paved coastal path starts at Will Rogers Beach in Santa Monica and passes through Venice, Hermosa and Redondo Beaches before ending at Torrance Beach. Rent a cruiser or an e-bike from **Joyride** (MAP: **2** P134 **B4**; *joyride santamonica.com; all-day rentals from $30*).

Ride the Waves with Poseidon
SURF SHOP

MAP: **3** P134 **C4**

Ever wondered what it feels like to be one of those bad-asses paddling the long board beyond the break and then riding the swell? Find out at **Poseidon** (*poseidonstandup.com*), a shop south of the pier. It sells and rents surfboards and stand-up paddleboards and can set you up with lessons, too.

Plunge into Annenberg Community Beach House
ACTIVITIES CENTER

MAP: **4** P134 **B1**

The **Annenberg Community Beach House** (*annenbergbeach house.com; parking $3/hr*) is a sleek and attractive city-owned beach activities center. Built on the estate of actress Marion Davies, this lavish facility is open to the public and has a lap pool, lounge chairs, yoga classes, beach volleyball, a fitness room and an art gallery. You can also tour the neoclassical Davies Guest House (p137).

Browse the Bergamot Station Arts Center
ART GALLERIES

MAP: **5** P134 **F4**

A former trolley yard, **Bergamot Station Arts Center** (*bergamotstation.com*) has been converted to one of LA's best arts centers. More than 20 private galleries show the works of well-regarded (and often famous) artists and photographers. The free exhibitions are always changing, so just wander around to see what's on. The Metro E Line stops right outside.

 THE 2025 PALISADES FIRE

From a small bush fire near Pacific Palisades on 7 January 2025, a combination of drought and high winds fueled an inferno that overwhelmed all efforts to contain it. Before the end of the month, it destroyed nearly 23,500 acres and over 6800 structures and killed at least 12 people. Much of the community of Pacific Palisades and parts of Malibu were destroyed. The fire reached the beaches, and entire swaths of the famous oceanfront homes along the Pacific Coast Hwy were destroyed. In the aftermath, the region struggled with recovery, cleanup and rebuilding.

See p134 for map of locations

Best Places for...

$ Budget $$ Midrange $$$ Top End

Eating

Casual Bites

Bay Cities Italian Deli & Bakery $

6 E3

The best Italian deli in LA, period. The signature sandwich is the spicy Godmother (piled with Italian meats), but there are plenty of other choices to complicate your decision. *9am-6pm Wed-Sun*

Holey Grail Donuts $

7 C7

Fab choice in a region known for great doughnuts. They're made with taro flour sourced from Hawai'i and then fried in coconut oil. Choose from over 60 flavors. *7am-7pm*

Sunny Blue $$

8 C8

In Japan, *omusubi* (rice balls, aka *onigiri*) are a staple. Fluffy rice is stuffed with fillings from seaweed to spicy salmon, then wrapped in *nori* (seaweed). Many veggie-friendly options. *11am-8pm*

Santa Monica Farmers Markets $

9 C2

Don't miss the markets, stocked with organic produce, flowers, baked goods and prepared foods. The big dog is the legendary Wednesday market; Saturday is a community scene. *8am-1pm Wed & Sat*

Relaxed Meals

Santa Monica Seafood $$

10 E1

One of SoCal's top seafood markets offers a tasty oyster bar and sit-down market cafe, where you can sample delicious chowder and more complex dishes. It's been in business since 1939. *9am-8pm*

Birdie G's $$

11 F4

Upscale comfort food with color and flair, and everything is served with down-home sensibility. There's a fun kids menu and even the dessert list is delightfully whimsical. It's close to the Bergamot Station Arts Center. *5-9pm*

Memorable Dining

Mélisse $$$

12 E1

Chef Josiah Citrin leads a superb kitchen team at this tasting room operating within his namesake one-star Citrin. Bookings are few, and bold flavors are melded with modern French recipes. *5:30-9pm Wed-Sat*

Éléphante $$$

13 C2

Grand ocean views from a breezy rooftop are the immediate draw. But the delectable small plates, pasta dishes and nicely charred pizzas will eventually draw your attention away from the palm-tree-fringed vistas. It's a stylish scene. *10am-midnight*

Drinking

Basic Drinks

Dogtown Coffee

14 C5

In the old Zephyr surf-shop headquarters, where skateboarding

EXPLORE

SANTA MONICA

was invented during the 1970s. It brews great coffee and makes a mean breakfast burrito. Fun fact: Dogtown was the boarders' nickname for southern Santa Monica and Venice. *7am-2pm*

Divine Vintage
 E1

Charming wine bar in a cute cottage. Most choices are organic. It's the perfect place for a mellow gathering with a friend. Nearby in this appealing strip on Montana Ave is Father's Office, a welcoming gastropub. *noon-8pm*

Bars with Appeal

Chez Jay
 C4

Since 1959, this nautical-themed dive has seen its share of Hollywood intrigue from the Rat Pack to the Brat Pack. It remains dark and dank inside (with seats outside); the classic steak and seafood menu's not bad. *2pm-midnight*

Bar Chloe
 C3

Cozy, dark and elegant, with dangling chandeliers, twinkling candles, intimate booths and crisp white tablecloths. The chamomile mai tai gets

rave reviews. It makes its own syrups and juices using farmers market produce. *6pm-midnight*

Library Alehouse
 C8

You can smell the sea at this Ocean Park gastropub where locals gather for beer and bites. Choose from a long list of local microbrews on tap while you hang on the cozy patio. *noon-11pm*

Penthouse
 C1

On the 18th floor of the Huntley Hotel is the highest bar on Santa Monica Bay, with sweeping views. There's a high-end food menu for hotel guests, but come to savor the vista while sipping a creative cocktail. *7am-11pm*

Shopping

Something for Everyone

Puzzle Zoo
 C3

Those searching galaxy-wide for the caped Lando Calrissian action figure, look no more. There's every figurine this side

of Endor. There's also an encyclopedic selection of puzzles, board games and toys. Kids (and many adults) adore it. *11am-7pm*

Jadis
 C8

A homespun, steampunk-paradise museum and shop grinding with old gears and spare-part robots, antique clocks, concept planes and cars, old globes and lanterns, many of which were film props. *11am-5pm Fri-Sun*

Ten Women Gallery
 C8

This longstanding gallery sells art, folk art and crafts from a cooperative of nearly three dozen female artists. Always changing, but look for works in ceramic, wood, textiles, jewelry and more. *10am-7pm*

Great Labels
 F1

Sensational secondhand couture and designer hand-me-downs from celebrity consigners. There are Oscar and Golden Globe gowns, elegant handbags, shoes and accessories from Pucci, Prada, Jimmy Choo and more. Breathtaking discounts. *11am-6pm*

★ WORTH A TRIP

Malibu

With the Pacific as the canvas, the oceanic spectacle extends along the Pacific Coast Hwy (PCH; Hwy 1) to Malibu, the fabled beach town. Although the entire region is working hard to recover from the devastating 2025 Palisades wildfires, there's much to engage the visitor.

MEALS WITH A VIEW

Beachfront legend **Duke's Malibu** employs minor local celebs, serving a rum cocktail-seafood-steak menu. The array of luxe Japanese joints includes the celeb-favored **Nobu Malibu** overlooking the glistening sea.

Scan this QR code for details on the Malibu area's parks, beaches and attractions.

Getty Villa

Just north of Santa Monica in Pacific Palisades is the remarkable **Getty Villa** *(getty.edu; free)*. It was built in 1974 when billionaire J Paul Getty decided to recreate Herculaneum's Villa dei Papiri, a Roman villa that was buried in the eruption of Mt Vesuvius in 79 CE. The focus here is on the art and cultures of ancient Greece, Rome and Etruria, and there's a vast collection of classical and Renaissance-era artworks on display. Corinthian columns surround perfectly manicured gardens and an elongated pool. Don't miss the Pompeii fountain and Temple of Herakles.

An advance, timed ticket is required; parking costs $25 ($15 after 3pm). Note: the **Getty Center** (p130) is one of LA's premier cultural highlights. The parking fee can be used at both on the same day.

Malibu Pier

Besides the extraordinary beaches, Malibu's one real highlight is its namesake wooden **pier**, which traces its history to 1905. Strolling its 700ft length is a delight. Some of the best views of the Malibu coast are from the pier, as the wall-to-wall beach houses (even after the 2025 fires destroyed so many) cut off views from the PCH.

The pier even has its own famous eatery, the **Malibu Farm Restaurant** *(9am-7pm)*.

GOODFOCUSED/SHUTTERSTOCK

Whitewashed dining rooms are perfect places for farm-to-table brunches, lunches and snacks.

Best Beaches

Park on the bluffs at **El Matador State Beach** and stroll down to sandstone rock towers rising from emerald coves. Dolphins breach the surface beyond the waves. Easily accessed from the PCH (and Metro bus), **Zuma Beach** has parking and long stretches of sand. Find privacy in the southeast at **Pirate's Cove**.

Where Malibu Creek meets the ocean, migratory birds proliferate at **Malibu Lagoon State Beach**, attracting human spotters. To the north are popular surf breaks. **Paradise Cove** is a famous semi-private beach controlled by a namesake cafe. Have lunch on the sand to avoid high parking fees. It was the setting for *The Rockford Files*.

GETTING THERE
Going north from Santa Monica, transit options dwindle to one Metro bus line, the 134 along the Pacific Coast Hwy to Malibu. There's a stop for the Getty Villa.

143

See p152
for eating,
drinking and
shopping
listings

Explore
Venice & South Coast Beaches

Researched by
Ryan Ver Berkmoes

Come down to the Boardwalk and inhale an incense-scented whiff of Venice, a boho beach town and longtime haven for artists, New Agers, road-weary tramps, skateboarders and free spirits. This is where Jim Morrison and the Doors lit their fire, Arnold Schwarzenegger pumped himself to stardom and Dennis Hopper finally settled down. Even as the famous canals gentrify, the Old Venice spirit endures.

Heading south, you pass through the string of South Bay beach towns for which LA is also famous. The long sandy swath never ends as you pass through one haven for volleyball and bacchanalia after another like Manhattan Beach.

Getting Around

 Public Transit
The Metro Rail E Line to Downtown Santa Monica is a nice beach stroll 1.5 miles north of Venice. Otherwise, take Metro Bus Line 33 and Santa Monica's Big Blue Bus Lines 1, 3 and 18 from the station south into Venice.

 Car
The South Bay beach towns have minimal bus service and are best reached by car, which also allows you to bounce between them along the Pacific Coast Hwy.

 Bike
Use the 22-mile-long Marvin Braude Bike Trail to cycle the entire coast.

★
THE BEST

SUNDAY AFTERNOON
Boardwalk drum
circle (p150)

———

WALK
Canals history (p151)

———

CREATIVE MOMENT Venice
Beach Art Walls (p149)

———

SWEET TREAT
Salt & Straw (p152)

———

SHOP
Venice Skateboarding
Stuff (p153)

Venice Boardwalk (p150)

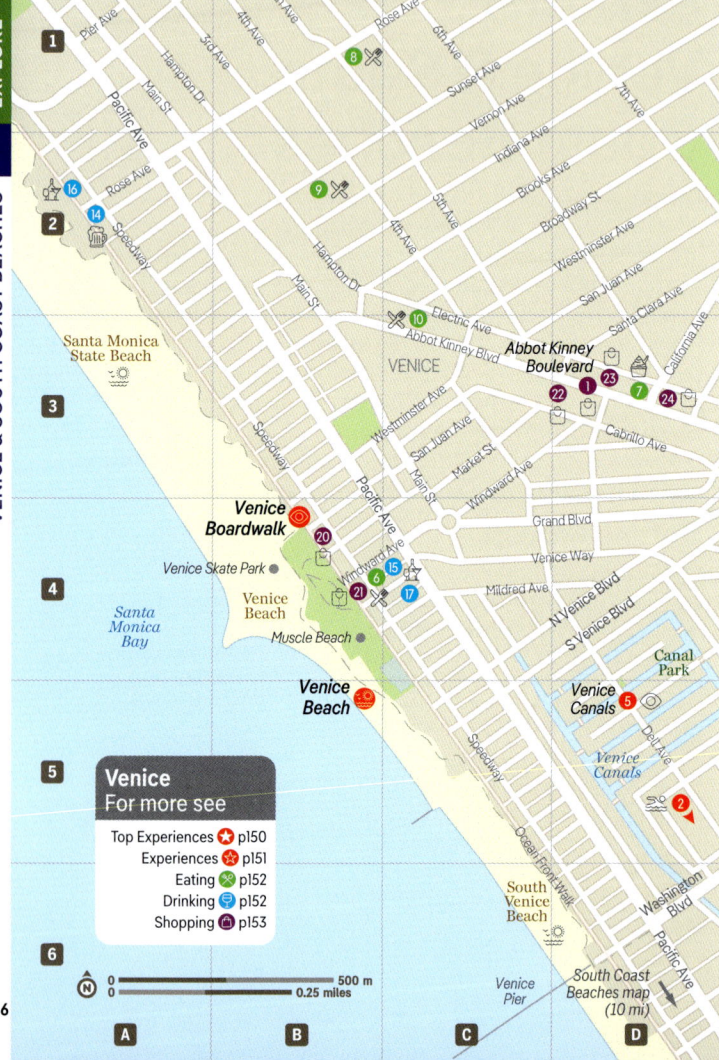

Venice Boardwalk

Abbot Kinney Boulevard

VENICE

Santa Monica State Beach

Santa Monica Bay

Venice Skate Park

Venice Beach

Muscle Beach

Venice Beach

Venice Canals

Canal Park

Venice Canals

South Venice Beach

Venice Pier

South Coast Beaches map (10 mi)

Venice
For more see

⭐ Top Experiences	p150
⭐ Experiences	p151
✖ Eating	p152
🍺 Drinking	p152
🛍 Shopping	p153

0   500 m
0   0.25 miles

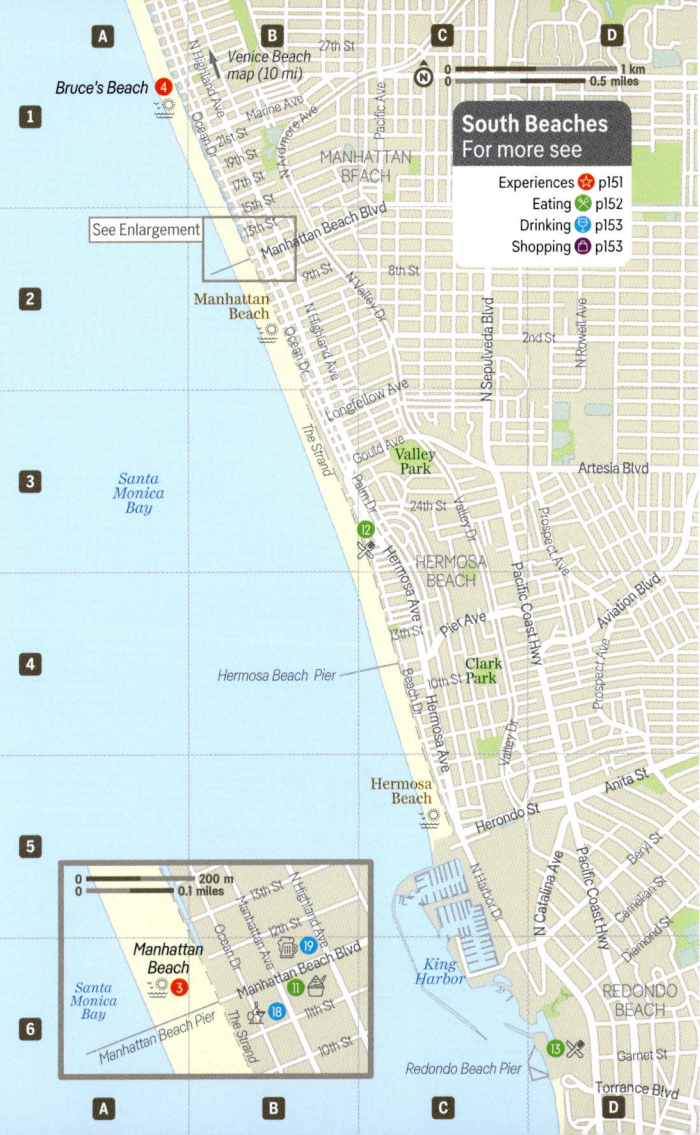

Bruce's Beach **4**

1

N High Ave
Ocean Dr
Venice Beach
map (10 mi)
27th St

Marine Ave
21st St
19th St
17th St
15th St

N Ardmore Ave

Pacific Ave

MANHATTAN
BEACH

0   1 km
0   0.5 miles

South Beaches
For more see

Experiences ✪ p151
Eating ✪ p152
Drinking ✪ p153
Shopping ✪ p153

See Enlargement

13th St
Manhattan Beach Blvd
11th St
9th St
8th St

N Valley Dr

2

Manhattan
Beach ✿

Ocean Dr
N Highland Ave
Longfellow Ave

N Sepulveda Blvd

2nd St

N Poinsettia Ave
N Rowell Ave

3

Santa
Monica
Bay

The Strand

Gould Ave
Palm Dr
24th St

**Valley
Park**

Prospect Ave

Artesia Blvd

N Valley Dr

12

Hermosa Ave
8th St

HERMOSA
BEACH

Pacific Coast Hwy

Aviation Blvd

4

Hermosa Beach Pier

Pier Ave
10th St

Beach Dr

**Clark
Park**

Hermosa Ave

Valley Dr

Anita St

5

Hermosa
Beach ✿

Herondo St

N Catalina Ave

Pacific Coast Hwy

Beryl St

Carnelian St
Diamond St

0   200 m
0   0.1 miles

13th St
N Highland Ave

Manhattan
Beach ✿ **3**

Santa
Monica
Bay

Ocean Ave
Manhattan Ave

12th St
Manhattan Beach Blvd

🏛 **19**

🍴 **11**

The Strand

Manhattan Beach Pier

11th St
18

10th St

N Harbor Dr

**King
Harbor**

REDONDO
BEACH

13 🍴

6

Redondo Beach Pier

Garnet St

Torrance Blvd

WALKING TOUR

Exploring Venice

Step into the Venice lifestyle – from the alternative to the nutty to the upscale – and see the creativity that helps give the area its idiosyncratic vibe. On this walk, you'll never stray far from the beach life, and the smell of the Pacific and the sound of its surf is always with you.

START	END	LENGTH
Venice Pier	Binoculars Building	2.5 miles; 2–3 hours

① Quiet Sands

Start at **Venice Pier**, where nature's golden sands unfurl and the blue sea churns. This is the quieter end of Venice Beach. The commercial strip and associated mania are north. Low-key, well-heeled beach houses are backed by the Marina del Rey, the 5000-slip artificial harbor, mall and condo development created from a salt marsh in the early 1960s.

② Canal Idyll

The idyllic **Venice Canals** neighborhood (p151) preserves 3 miles of waterways connected by bridges where ducks preen, artists paint and locals lollygag in rowboats or sip cocktails on little barges moored in front of their cute homes. It's shrunk in size over time, but what's left – six canals – is worth wandering. Exit the enclave and turn left on N Venice Blvd.

③ High-End Gallery

Pause at **LA Louver** (lalouver.com; free), a contemporary art gallery with museum-quality exhibitions. It represents dozens of big-name artists, including Dale Chihuly, David Hockney and Ed and Nancy Kienholz. Since 1994 it's been housed in this landmark cubist building designed by Frederick Fisher.

④ LA Woman's Start

Now it's time for the main event, the Venice Boardwalk, where free expression is de rigueur. Look for Rip Cronk's epic 30ft-tall **Jim Morrison Mural** on your right. In 1965 Morrison was crashing at his friend Ray Manzarek's Venice apartment and they plotted to start the Doors.

⑤ Sanctioned Graffiti

Angle across the sand to the **Venice Beach Art Walls** (veniceartwalls. com), a vortex for the loony, the free-spirited and the hip. The tagged-up towers and the free-standing concrete walls have been covered by graffiti painters since 1961. You can join in on weekends – apply to the public foundation that maintains the walls for a free permit.

⑥ Soaring Murals

Head away from the sand briefly on Windward Ave until you see **Venice Reconstituted**, a Cronk ode to Botticelli's *Birth of Venus*. Witty takes on famous artworks are a recurring theme in Venice murals. Continuing north, nose around the narrow lanes and alleys just off the walk between Wavecrest Ave and Brooks Ave, another area rich with ever-changing murals.

⑦ See the Binoculars

To see what happens when creativity is monetized, walk inland three blocks on Rose Ave to the **Binoculars Building**, which was originally (1991) the headquarters for the Chiat/Day advertising agency. This Frank Gehry–designed office building is now a Google office, Claes Oldenburg and Coosje van Bruggen sculpture out front and all.

⭐ **TOP EXPERIENCE**

Venice's Beach & Boardwalk

Prepare for a sensory overload at Venice's **Boardwalk** and **Beach**, one of LA's essential experiences. Buff bodybuilders brush elbows with street performers and sellers of sunglasses, ribald underwear and cannabis, while cyclists and in-line skaters whiz by and skateboarders and graffiti sprayers get their own domains.

MAP P146 **B4** and **B5**

PLANNING TIP
Venice's beach and boardwalk are Southern California's second most popular attractions after Disneyland®, getting 10 million visitors a year. The busiest times are weekend afternoons in summer.

Scan this QR code for practical details about Venice Beach.

Boardwalk Zeitgeist

Life on the Venice Boardwalk moves to a different rhythm. It's a wacky carnival alive with Hula-Hoop magicians, jazz combos, Barbie wannabes, garage rockers and artists (good and bad). The Sunday-afternoon **drum circle** draws hundreds of revelers for jamming and spontaneous dancing on the grassy mounds (and sometimes on the sand). In-line skaters and cyclists are thwarted on summer weekends.

Beach Cultures

Venice's beach has the same powdery sand that makes LA's 20-plus miles of shore so vaunted. What's different here is the culture. Yes, there are the famous **Art Walls** (p149), but there's also a whole panoply of cultures with their own patch of sand. Gym rats with an exhibitionist streak can get a tan and workout at famous **Muscle Beach**, the outdoor gym right between the sand and boardwalk. There are also **volleyball nets** and **basketball courts**.

Skate Park Show

When Angelenos drained their swimming pools during a 1970s drought, board-toting teens made their not-quite-welcome invasion and modern skateboarding culture was born. Today the beach's public, 17,000-sq-ft, ocean-view **skate park** is a destination for both high flyers and gawking spectators. There are regular competitions, and the spectacle is world-class.

EXPERIENCES

Shop Trendy Venice
BOUTIQUES

MAP: **1** P146 **D3**

The mile-long strip of **Abbot Kinney Boulevard** between Venice Blvd and Main St is lined with upscale boutiques (both indie and chain), galleries, lofts and cafes and restaurants. Many shops are housed in reconstructed beach cottages. The parallel stretch of **Lincoln Boulevard** four blocks north is also good shopping territory.

Get Active on Sand, Sea & Air
GEAR RENTAL AND ACTIVITIES

MAP: **2** P146 **D5**

You're never far from places to rent gear at Venice. You'll find businesses out on the sand in huts and all along the boardwalk. Items on offer include bikes, surfboards, boogie boards, lounging chairs and umbrellas.

Immediately south, **Marina Del Rey Parasailing** (*marinadel reyparasailing.com*) will have you flying 500ft high or higher. The views can be stunning.

Enjoy Manhattan Beach
BEACH TOWN

The birthplace of beach volleyball, **Manhattan Beach** (MAP: **3** P147 **A6**) may have gone chic, but that salty-dog heart still beats, and Downtown's trendy restaurants and boutiques mix with dive bars.

Ditch your shoes on the sweep of golden sand. You'll find pick-up **volleyball courts**, a **pier** with sweeping views, and a consistent sandy bottom.

Founded in 1912, **Bruce's Beach** (MAP: **4** P147 **A1**) was a popular private African American beach. Driven by racism, the town of Manhattan Beach seized the beach from the Bruce family in 1924. In 2022, LA County returned the area bounded by Highland Ave and 27th St to the family, who then sold it back to the county so it can continue to serve as a popular public park.

CANAL STORIES

MAP: **5** P146 **D5**

The picturesque **Venice Canals** were created in 1905 by developer and conservationist Abbot Kinney, who wanted to replicate Italy's famed waterways, dubbing the area the 'Venice of America.' Having become decrepit after WWII, the canals have reclaimed their beauty and charm, especially with the architecturally diverse homes that line the canalside paths.

A popular film and TV location, the canals' Hollywood apex may have been toward the end of *Touch of Evil* (1958), when a dissolute Orson Wells dies flopping around in the then-polluted waters.

Best Places for...

$** Budget **$$** Midrange **$$$ Top End

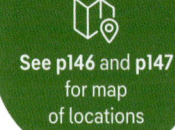

See **p146** and **p147**
for map
of locations

Eating

Great Venice Choices

Teddy's Red Tacos $
6 P146 **B4**

Birria had its trendy moment, but it remains a foundational element of Mexican cuisine. Teddy's does the long-simmered, piquant Mexican stew better than nearly anyone. Enjoy tacos and platters at the outdoor tables. *10am-10pm*

Salt & Straw $
7 P146 **D3**

There's always a line out the door at this Abbot Kinney Blvd ice-cream fantasy land. Adventurous, seasonally themed flavors change monthly. *11am-11pm*

Café Gratitude $$
8 P146 **B1**

Cutting-edge vegan dishes are paired with a patio and fresh sea breezes. It's sustainable, locavore, organic and always surprising. *10am-9pm*

Gjusta $$
9 P146 **B2**

Very local bakery, cafe and deli behind a nondescript storefront on a hidden side street. Expect to be surprised by the combinations of flavors and inventive presentation. Great patio. Food to go is ideal for picnics. *7am-4pm*

Felix Trattoria $$$
10 P146 **C3**

People flock here for maestro chef Evan Funke's *rigatoni all'amatriciana*, or some artfully invented new form of pasta – often created right before your eyes. Superb seasonal ingredients. *5-9:30pm*

South Bay Bites

Manhattan Beach Creamery $
11 P147 **B6**

House-made ice creams are served in cones or pressed between two cookies for a 'Cream'wich' – get the strawberry shortcake. Cases of brownies, cookies, cupcakes and chocolate-covered bananas make the line worth it. *10am-9pm*

Martha's Hermosa Beach $
12 P147 **C3**

Beachside patio joint is a good first stop before a day on the sand. Residents swear by the egg dishes like omelets and Benedicts. Sandwiches include Vegas favorite the Monte Cristo. *7am-3pm*

Quality Seafood $$
13 P147 **D6**

Since 1953 the Redondo pier has been home to this big seafood market. Huge selection of fresh fish, oysters and crabs caught in the harbor, and they'll cook it your way. *10:30am-8pm*

Drinking

Venice Imbibing

Venice Ale House
14 P146 **A2**

Boardwalk seating at Venice's northern end, blessed with a welcoming patio for sunset people-watching. Long boards suspended from the rafters, beachy tunes, plenty of local brews on tap and organic bar chow. *11:30am-8pm*

Townhouse & Del Monte Speakeasy

15 P146 **C4**

Upstairs, a cool, dark bar with a history that twists and turns back to 1915; downstairs, a speakeasy, where DJs spin, comics take the mike and jazz players jam. A good time almost any night. *5pm-2am*

Waterfront

16 P146 **A2**

Ideally suited for the boardwalk, an indoor-outdoor beach bar that's a magnet for hipsters, surfers and shamblers, who all rub elbows while quaffing beers, wines and coffees. Decent food too. *11am-9pm*

High Rooftop Lounge

17 P146 **C4**

Venice's most popular rooftop bar boasts 360-degree views from its sprawling 5th-floor location. Inventive seasonal cocktails and small dishes to keep you sated between rounds. Always a good scene; be sure to book in summer. *noon-10pm*

Manhattan Beach Bars

Ercoles 1101

18 P147 **B6**

Funky counterpoint to stylish bars. A dark,

chipped, well-irrigated dive with a barn door open to everyone from salty barflies to Gen Z pub crawlers and volleyball stars. Beloved since 1927. *10am-2am*

Simmzy's

19 P147 **B6**

A terrific gastropub with dozens of beers on tap, reasonably priced wines and the sorts of cocktails you dream about while prone on the sand. The covered deck facing the street is ideal for people-watching. *11am-10pm*

Shopping

Boardwalk Finds

Small World Books

20 P146 **B4**

Get your best beach read here. Tucked behind a cafe, this used and new bookstore has fab staff recommendations and an appealing and eclectic selection. *10am-8pm*

Venice Skateboarding Stuff

21 P146 **B4**

Jammed in amid the usual schmeer of nonsensical stores selling tat, this store deals quality gear in

the foundational land of skateboarding. It reps all the best brands and has expertise going back to 1998. *10am-6pm*

Abbot Kinney Boulevard Choices

Aviator Nation

22 P146 **D3**

This beachwear brand's original store sells coastal-chic hoodies, tees and blankets. Behind the store is an awesome chill space with a DJ station and games, all done up in the brand's trademark yellow, orange and red stripes. *10am-9pm*

Principessa

23 P146 **D3**

Affordable boutique with sporty denim and skirts, jewelry and droopy hats, baby-doll dresses, scarves, sequined boots and purses. In case you need some holiday essentials, they've got sleek swimsuits and negligees, too. *11am-7pm*

Burro

24 P146 **D3**

An Abbot Kinney fave, Burro deals in quality aromatherapy candles, art books, a smattering of boho-chic women's attire, creative stationery, fair-trade beach bags from India and beaded jewelry. *10:30am-6pm*

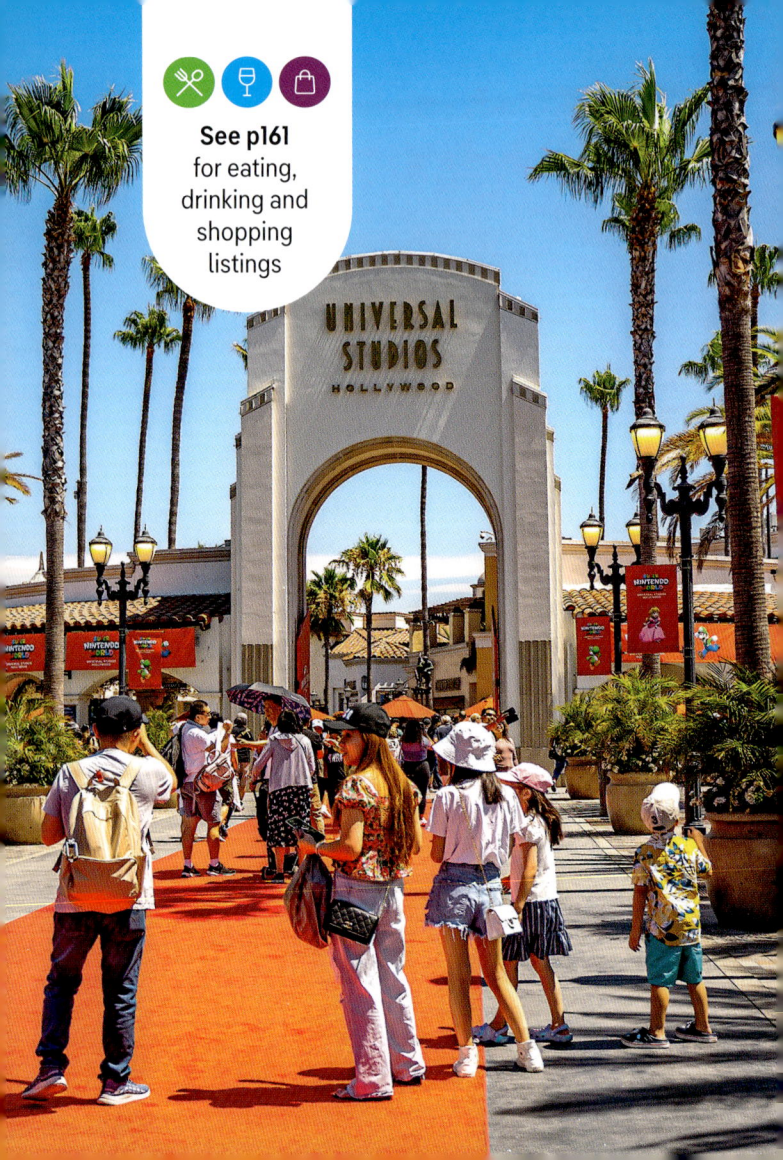

See p161
for eating,
drinking and
shopping
listings

Explore
Burbank &
Universal City

*Researched by
Ryan Ver Berkmoes*

Angelenos from the other side of the Hollywood Hills think of two things when it comes to 'the Valley': major studios and urban sprawl. One, they think, is worth visiting; the other, not so much.

Snootiness aside, the Valley (principally the communities of – roughly west to east – Sherman Oaks, Studio City, Universal City, North Hollywood, Burbank and Glendale) does sprawl. It's the place where car culture was invented. But look closer and you'll see plenty of other culture, such that North Hollywood has its own arts district ('NoHo'). Of the studios, one offers an excellent tour and the other comprises a major theme park.

Getting Around

 Metro

Take the Metro B Line from Downtown LA and Hollywood to the Universal City/Studio City and North Hollywood stations. The former has shuttle buses up the steep hill to the Universal Studios theme park.

 Car

Much of the San Fernando Valley is flat, but it defines suburbia and is so spread out that there are few areas that are worth walking. When Dionne Warwick sang 'LA is a great big freeway...,' she could have been describing the Valley.

THE BEST

THEME PARK Universal Studios Hollywood (p158)

———

STUDIO TOUR Warner Bros Studio Tour (p160)

———

DINING STRIP Studio City Sushi Row (p161)

———

SNACK Big Pink doughnut at Universal (p158)

———

SHOP It's a Wrap! (p161)

Universal Studios Hollywood (p158)
IV-OLGA/SHUTTERSTOCK

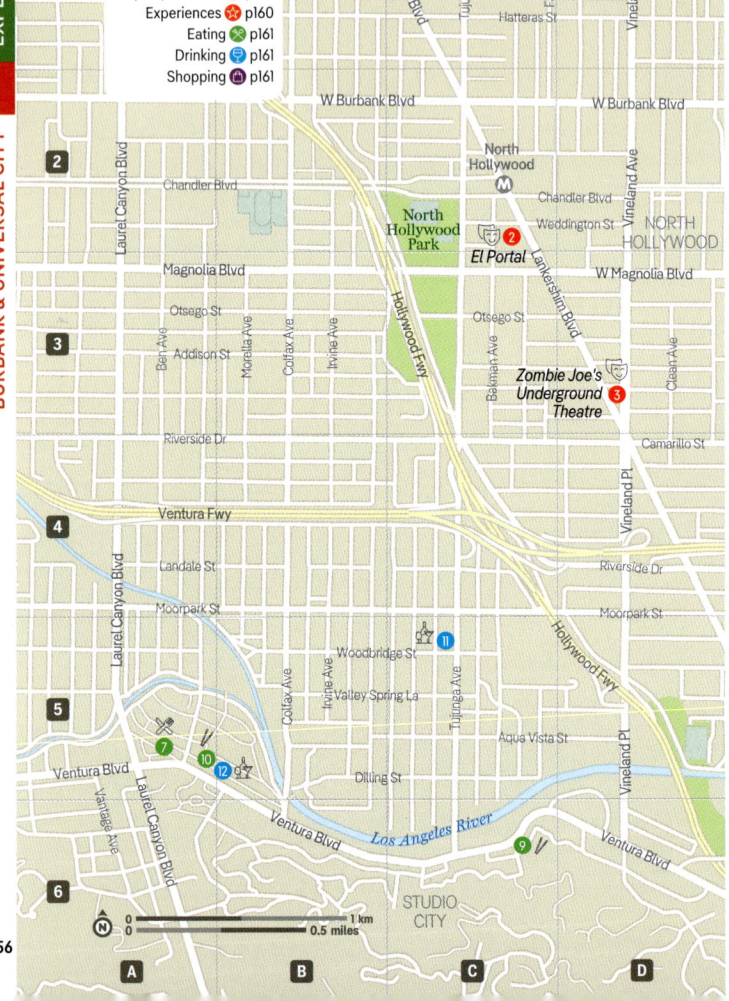

For more see

Top Experiences ⭐ p158
Experiences ⭐ p160
Eating ✹ p161
Drinking ◉ p161
Shopping 🛍 p161

Oxnard St

Lankershim Blvd

Tujunga Ave

Fair Ave

Vineland Ave

Hatteras St

W Burbank Blvd

W Burbank Blvd

North
Hollywood Ⓜ

Laurel Canyon Blvd

Chandler Blvd

Chandler Blvd

Weddington St

NORTH
HOLLYWOOD

North
Hollywood
Park

El Portal ❷

Lankershim Blvd

Vineland Ave

Magnolia Blvd

W Magnolia Blvd

Otsego St

Otsego St

Ben Ave

Addison St

Morella Ave

Colfax Ave

Irvine Ave

Balsam Ave

Clean Ave

Hollywood Fwy

Zombie Joe's
Underground
Theatre ❸

Riverside Dr

Camarillo St

Ventura Fwy

Vineland Pl

Riverside Dr

Laurel Canyon Blvd

Landale St

Moorpark St

Moorpark St

Hollywood Fwy

Woodbridge St ⑪

Irvine Ave

Tujunga Ave

Valley Spring La

Aqua Vista St

Vineland Pl

Colfax Ave

⑦

⑩

⑫

Ventura Blvd

Dilling St

Vantage Ave

Laurel Canyon Blvd

Ventura Blvd

Ventura Blvd

Los Angeles River

⑨

Ventura Blvd

STUDIO
CITY

N

0   1 km
0   0.5 miles

Oxnard St

Hatteras St

Cahuenga Blvd

Clybourn Ave

Edison Blvd

N Hollywood Way

W Burbank Blvd

MAGNOLIA PARK

N Keystone St

N Buena Vista St

N Frederic St

N Florence St

N Niagara St

Chandler Blvd

Whitnall Hwy

N Hollywood Way

N Pass Ave

Clybourn Ave

13

W Magnolia Blvd

N California St

N Lima St

Clark Ave

Chandler Blvd

Cahuenga Blvd

W Magnolia Blvd

Clark Ave

Addison St

W Verdugo Ave

Verdugo Park

W Verdugo Ave

BURBANK

N California St

N Niagara St

Camarillo St

Ledge Ave

Forman Ave

Clybourn Ave

N Pass Ave

N Hollywood Way

N Avon St

W Olive Ave

W Alameda Ave

Cahuenga Blvd

Ventura Fwy

Riverside Dr

5

Olive Ave

Ventura Fwy

Warner Bros
Studio Tour

Pass Ave

Warner Bros
Studios

Lankershim Blvd

Ledge Ave

Forman Ave

Valley Spring La

Toluca
Lake

Lakeside
Country Club

8

Los Angeles River

Forest Lawn Dr

Griffith
Park

Hollywood Fwy

Universal City/
Studio City

Universal
Studios
Hollywood

UNIVERSAL
CITY

Barham Blvd

Burbank
Peak
(1690ft)

4 Baked Potato

157

★ **TOP EXPERIENCE**

Universal Studios Hollywood

Although Universal is one of the world's oldest continuously operating studios (since 1912), it's best known for its movie-themed parks. The original park now all but overwhelms the original studio in North Hollywood and is a hugely popular attraction with its thrill rides and live-action shows.

MAP P156 **F6**

PLANNING TIP
Buy tickets online for possible savings. Also, the park can reach capacity and the ticket booths close. Watch for two-for-one offers, which give you free admission on a second non-consecutive day.

Scan this QR code for full details and to buy tickets.

The Main Events

Officially known as **Universal Studios Hollywood**, to differentiate it from the other parks around the globe (all of which are much larger, if you're an aficionado), the park is home to such popular rides as the **Flight of the Hippogriff** roller coaster and the 3-D **Harry Potter and the Forbidden Journey**. Buy wizarding equipment and 'every-flavour' beans in the fantasy-themed shops, then quaff mugs of butterbeer at **Three Broomsticks restaurant**.

In **Super Nintendo World**, the big ride is **Mario Kart: Bowser's Challenge**, which uses virtual reality to put riders inside the game. Elsewhere, the **Jurassic World** ride is a float back to dinosaur days before a tumble through a land of raptors and T rexes. A ride based on **The Simpsons** rockets along through Springfield.

Other Park Attractions

The park also includes the original **tram tour of the studio backlot**, although over the years this has morphed into more of a theme-park ride than an actual behind-the-scenes tour.

Flashing video screens, oversized facades and garish color combos animate **Universal CityWalk**, the outdoor shopping concourse adjacent to Universal Studios. Under the glitz, CityWalk's shops and restaurants are meant to echo the themes inside

V_E/SHUTTERSTOCK

the park, with a few familiar brands thrown in. The **Hello Kitty and Friends Cafe** is a hit.

Practicalities

Budget a full day to enjoy the park, especially in summer. Universal Studios Hollywood uses demand pricing, which varies significantly throughout the year. At non-peak times, one-day admission is adult/child $109/103. At peak times, such as school holidays, it's $154/148.

You can cut the often long lines for rides at busy times by purchasing an Express Pass one-day admission for a significant premium: $329 in peak periods. Extras can add up quickly. Parking is $35 to $75, depending on how close you are to the entrance. Avoid the charges and traffic by taking the Metro B Line to Universal City/Studio City and then the free shuttle.

QUICK BREAK
Among the plethora of food options, **the Lard Lad** doughnut stand in the Simpsons Springfield area gets raves. The Big Pink is 8in of creamy frosting and rainbow sprinkles.

EXPERIENCES

Tour Warner Bros Studios

STUDIO TOUR

MAP: **1** P156 **H4**

The **Warner Bros Studio Tour** (*wbstudiotour.com; tours adult/child from $76/65*) offers a fun, mostly authentic look behind the scenes of a major studio. Much of the lot dates to 1926, and large parts of it feel unchanged since the days when Jack Warner was cutting deals.

The two-hour standard tour kicks off with a video of WB's greatest hits (*Rebel Without a Cause,* many *Batmans* etc), before a tram whisks you around 110 acres of soundstages, legacy sets for TV shows like *Friends* and *The Big Bang Theory* and technical departments, including props, costumes and a collection of Batmobiles. It's awe-inspiring as you encounter the soundstages where *The Big Sleep, Blade Runner* and *La La Land* were shot.

Tour variations include the recommended **TCM Classic Films Tour** (*adult/child $99/85*), focusing on the studio's history and production of films like *Casablanca*. The six-hour **Deluxe Tour** (*$330*) goes more in-depth and includes lunch.

Enjoy Nightlife in the Valley

LIVE PERFORMANCE

The **NoHo** (aka North Hollywood) **Arts District** along Lankershim Blvd is sprinkled with theaters and venues known for their edgy live performances, music and comedy.

Dating to 1926, **El Portal** (MAP: **2** P156 **C2**; *elportaltheatre.com*) is a three-stage mainstay with top-name acts. **Zombie Joe's Underground Theatre** (MAP: **3** P156 **D3**; *zombiejoes. com*) is part theater, part haunted house. Shows are by turns creepy, campy, deranged and critically lauded.

A bit south, **Baked Potato** (MAP: **4** P156 **E6**; *thebakedpotato.com*) is an intimate jazz-and-blues hall – LA's oldest – where the schedule mixes no-names with big-timers.

GUIDE TO STUDIO TOURS

Four out of LA's five surviving major studios offer regular public tours (Disney doesn't). Besides Warner Bros, there are the following:

Paramount Pictures (p47)

MAP: P40 **F6**

Unfussy tours of the deeply historic Hollywood lot, which is pretty quiet these days.

Sony Pictures (p111)

MAP: P110

Covers what was once MGM Studios; there's not an overwhelming sense of history with all the intellectual rights musical chairs.

Universal Studios (p158)

MAP: P156 **F6**

Turned its tours into a theme park by the 1970s. The 'backlot' really isn't, but it's a spectacle.

Best Places for...

$ Budget $$ Midrange $$$ Top End

See p156 for map of locations

Eating
Our Picks

Bob's Big Boy $
 G4

Famous survivor of once-ubiquitous chain of diners renowned for a winsome mascot. There's Googie architecture extraordinaire at this rendition that dates to 1949, plus boffo nighttime neon. *6am-midnight*

Chili John's $
6 H1

Seen in *Once Upon a Time in Hollywood,* this institution has been dishing up chili around a U-shaped counter since 1946. It's mostly over spaghetti, but also chili dogs, the sloppy john sandwich (a joe but with chili) and more. *11am-7pm*

Tuning Fork LA $$
7 A5

Has a music-industry vibe (CBS Studios are down the block) and staff spin tunes most nights. Casual bistro defines the California cuisine ethos: fresh, simple and creative. Good wine and beer list. *5-9:30pm*

Smoke House $$
8 G5

Steakhouse right outside Warner Bros that's been serving luminaries since 1948. Legend has it George Clooney starting his production company here while he was shooting *ER*. Top spot for cocktails. *11:30am-10pm*

Studio City Sushi Row

Daichan $$
9 C6

Stuffed with knickknacks, pasted with posters and staffed by a sunny owner-operator, this offbeat, homestyle Japanese diner in an unassuming minimall offers some of the best (and tastiest) local deals. *11:30am-2:30pm & 5:30-8:30pm Mon-Sat*

Asanebo $$
10 A5

In a strip mall, this stylish standout has dishes such as halibut sashimi with fresh truffle, and *kanpachi* (amberjack) with miso and serrano chilies. Gracious staff. *5-10pm*

Drinking
Studio City

Velvet Martini Lounge
11 C5

Sophisticated spot with a mid-century vibe. Cocktails and sometimes a jazzy combo or a classic film. Food from Vitello's Restaurant out front. *6-10pm*

Black Market Liquor Bar
12 B5

Under a vaulted ceiling in dark and moody surrounds, this upscale tavern has a menu of unusual cocktails and beers. *5-10pm*

Shopping
Film & TV Costumes

It's a Wrap!
13 G2

Outlet used to unload on-screen wardrobes and props. Great prices on designer labels. Items are racked by show affiliation. Costumes from productions on display near Halloween. *10:30am-6pm*

Disneyland® Resort

Possibly California's most iconic sight, Walt Disney's illustrious creation is the self-dubbed 'Happiest Place on Earth.' The streets here are always clean, employees (aka 'cast members') are always upbeat and parades happen every day. Since opening in 1955, the ever-growing Disneyland® has delighted hundreds of millions of people.

GETTING THERE
Anaheim is 25 miles southeast of Downtown LA via I-5. Amtrak or Metrolink trains from LA stop at Anaheim's ARTIC transit center, a short shuttle to Disneyland® on bus 14 or 15.

Scan this QR code for all official details and to buy tickets and passes.

Disneyland® Park

Leave SoCal behind and enter **Main Street USA**, an idealized turn-of-the-20th-century town fashioned after Walt's hometown of Marceline, MO. The steam **Disneyland® Railroad** circles the perimeter, providing a great intro to the park.

Controversially, in 2025 **Great Moments with Mr Lincoln**, the 15-minute audio-animatronic show with Honest Abe spouting bromides, was partly replaced by **Walt Disney – A Magical Life**, in which a robotic Walt talks about his vision for Disneyland® and sings a song.

Star Wars: Galaxy's Edge

Inside Disneyland®'s largest land (14 acres), the mega-popular **Star Wars: Rise of the Resistance** puts you in an immersive adventure. Nearby are opportunities to make your own light saber or droid, or visit **Oga's Cantina**, modeled after the inside of Jabba's Palace. Fans of the movies will enjoy just wandering around, marveling at Disney's attention to detail.

Tomorrowland

The 1950s imagineers' vision of the future could now be called Mid-Century Land. **Venerable Space Mountain** remains one of the USA's best roller

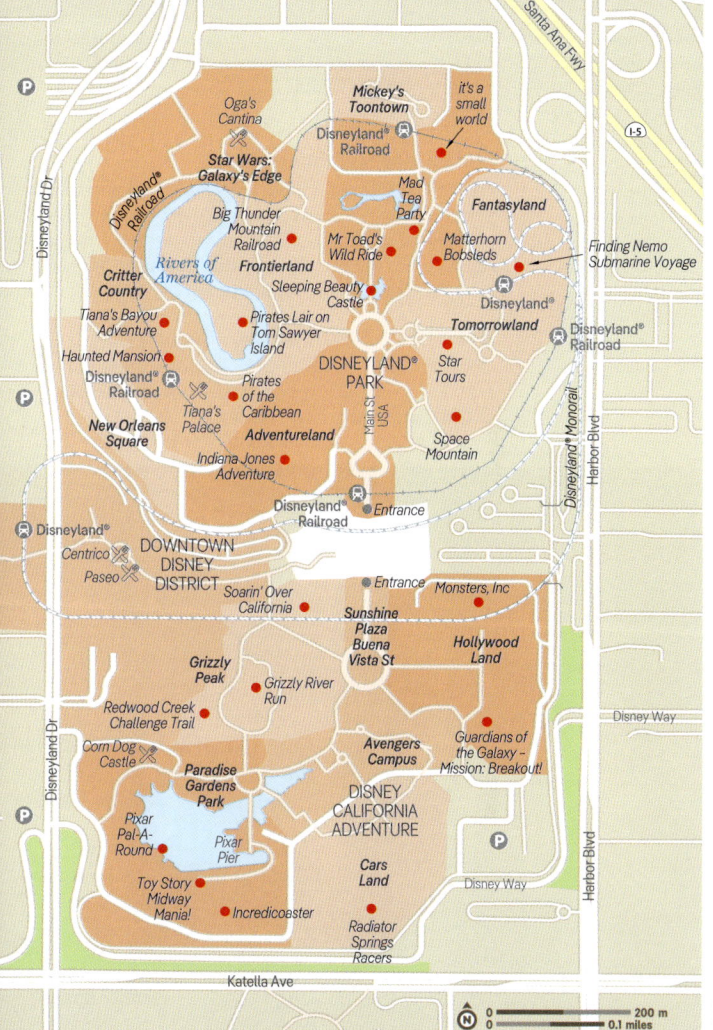

Santa Ana Fwy

I-5

Oga's Cantina

Mickey's Toontown

it's a small world

Disneyland® Railroad

Star Wars: Galaxy's Edge

Disneyland® Railroad

Big Thunder Mountain Railroad

Mad Tea Party

Fantasyland

Matterhorn Bobsleds

Finding Nemo Submarine Voyage

Mr Toad's Wild Ride

Rivers of America

Frontierland

Sleeping Beauty Castle

Critter Country

Tiana's Bayou Adventure

Pirates Lair on Tom Sawyer Island

Tomorrowland

Disneyland®

Disneyland® Railroad

Haunted Mansion

DISNEYLAND® PARK

Star Tours

Disneyland® Railroad

Pirates of the Caribbean

Main St USA

New Orleans Square

Tiana's Palace

Adventureland

Space Mountain

Indiana Jones Adventure

Disneyland® Railroad

Entrance

Disneyland®

Disneyland® Monorail

Harbor Blvd

DOWNTOWN DISNEY DISTRICT

Centrico Paseo

Entrance

Soarin' Over California

Monsters, Inc

Sunshine Plaza Buena Vista St

Hollywood Land

Grizzly Peak

Grizzly River Run

Redwood Creek Challenge Trail

Disney Way

Corn Dog Castle

Avengers Campus

Guardians of the Galaxy – Mission: Breakout!

Paradise Gardens Park

DISNEY CALIFORNIA ADVENTURE

Disneyland Dr

Pixar Pal-A-Round

Pixar Pier

Cars Land

Toy Story Midway Mania!

Incredicoaster

Radiator Springs Racers

Disney Way

Harbor Blvd

Katella Ave

0   200 m
0   0.1 miles
N

coasters, hurtling you into complete darkness at great speed. For retro high-tech, the **monorail** glides to Tomorrowland from Downtown Disney and the hotels.

Fantasyland & Frontierland

Fantasyland is best known for **it's a small world**, a boat ride past hundreds of audio-animatronic international children singing an earworm of a theme song. Thrills are provided by **Big Thunder Mountain Railroad**, a mining-themed roller coaster.

New Orleans Square & Bayou Country

Honoring Walt's favorite city, New Orleans Square captures a slice of French Quarter charm. **Pirates of the Caribbean** is the second-longest ride in Dis-

TAKE A BREAK
There's food of all kinds inside the parks; for a change, Downtown Disney offers dining before, during or after your visit. Use your ticket for re-entry to the parks.

SEAN TEEGARDEN/DISNEYLAND RESORT

neyland® (17 minutes) and provided inspiration for the popular movies. The water ride **Tiana's Bayou Adventure** (pictured left), inspired by *The Princess and the Frog*, opened in 2024. **Tiana's Palace** is popular for its authentic New Orleans cuisine.

Adventureland

The hands-down highlight here is the safari-style **Indiana Jones Adventure**. Cool down on the purposely hokey **Jungle Cruise**. The **Enchanted Tiki Room** features a campy show of singing, dancing birds and flowers. Skip the overhyped Dole Whips.

Parades, Fireworks & Live Entertainment

There are daily parades in Disneyland® and Disney California Adventure (DCA), with floats accompanied by Disney tunes and costumed characters. Don't miss DCA's premier show, the 22-minute **World of Color** firework spectacular. Check the app for info on more live acts and shows.

Disney California Adventure Park

Across the plaza from Disneyland®, **Disney California Adventure** (opened in 2001) is an ode to the state with an overlay of Disney intellectual property. Covering more acres than Disneyland®, DCA feels less crowded than Disneyland® Park.

Hollywood Land & Avengers Campus

It's Hollywood in miniature, with soundstages, movable props and – of course – a studio store. **Guardians of the Galaxy – Mission: Breakout!** is the most popular thrill ride, a tower with drops of 130ft.

Grizzly Peak

Grizzly Peak is DCA's salute to natural California. The superb **Grizzly River Run** takes you 'rafting' down a faux Sierra Nevada river – you will get wet. Kids can tackle the **Redwood Creek Challenge Trail**, with its 'Big Sir' redwoods. If you're hungry, the

DISNEYLAND®'S THREE AREAS
The resort consists of the original Disneyland® Park; the newer Disney California Adventure Park (DCA); and Downtown Disney District, an outdoor mall.

DISNEYLAND®'S FUTURE
Big changes are coming to Disneyland®. DCA will get a Coco-themed water ride and the Avengers Campus will get a marquee ride, Avengers Infinity Defense. Longer term, the Disneyland® Resort may expand by 50% after Orange County approved zoning changes.

ADMISSION PRICES

Pricing is based on demand. Many websites track admission prices; typically, Tuesday followed by Wednesday are the cheapest days and September is the cheapest month. Daily basic admission ranges from $110 to $210 before add-ons.

ESSENTIAL APP

Use the Disneyland® app to buy admission tickets and add-ons, check ride status, make Lightning Lane and dining reservations, check parade times etc. You'll use it more than you'd like to.

Corn Dog Castle has a grab-and-go hot link corn dog that's the best in the parks.

Cars Land

This land gets kudos for its detailed design based on the popular Disney Pixar *Cars* movies. Top billing goes to the **Radiator Springs Racers**, a race-car ride that jumps around a track decked out like a cartoon American West.

Pixar Pier

Looking like an amalgam of California's beachside amusement parks, Pixar Pier (pictured right) has the scream-inducing **Incredicoaster** and the 4D **Toy Story Midway Mania!**, where you earn points by target-shooting while your carnival car careens through an old-fashioned arcade with nods to the park's 70th.

Downtown Disney District

Connecting Disneyland®'s parks and hotels, this open-air, admission-free pedestrian mall bursts with opportunities to drop cash in stores, restaurants and entertainment venues. It's worth booking ahead for three of the restaurants: **Paseo** and **Centrico**, both created by chef Carlos Gaytan, the first Michelin-star-awarded chef born in Mexico; and **Din Tai Fung**, a branch of the popular original.

Lines & Waiting Times

Lines for Disneyland® Resort rides and attractions can be interminably long, but the Lightning Lane (LL) can make your visit more efficient – at a cost.

The LL Multi Pass is good for one use on most rides for one day. The LL Single Pass is just that. Buy them in advance or once you're in the parks through the app. Use LL to reserve entrance times for popular rides and attractions, which can reduce your waiting times. However, like many aspects of a Magic Kingdom visit, the scheme is overly complex.

CHRISTIAN THOMPSON/DISNEYLAND RESORT

Once inside the parks, you can start reserving entrance times, but you can only do so after each ride, so you can't plan your day all at once. Also, the gaps in reserving may result in dead time between rides, leaving you with nothing to do but shop. People complain that they spend much of their time inside the parks on their phones trying to reserve times.

Use the LL at rides where you've reserved a spot, bypassing the people in the regular line, although you still may end up waiting.

Like admission tickets, LL has demand-based pricing *(from $25 per person)*. The most popular rides (eg Star Wars: Rise of the Resistance) are not in the LL Multi Pass scheme; for these you need an additional LL Single Pass *(from $25)*.

There's now a LL Premier Pass. Sold for several hundred dollars in limited quantities in advance through the app, it allows users to use the LL lanes without reserving times on their phones.

PARKING
Parking costs $35 a day; the extra charge for Preferred Parking yields little benefit. Of the various ginormous parking structures, Pixar Pals puts you a pleasant stroll away from the parks, saving the need to line up for shuttles.

Los Angeles Toolkit

Family Travel 170

Accommodations 171

Food, Drink & Nightlife 172

LGBTQ+ Travelers 174

Health & Safe Travel 175

Responsible Travel 176

Accessible Travel 178

Nuts & Bolts 179

Tail o' the Pup (p128)
AMELIA MULARZ/LONELY PLANET

Family Travel

LA is a tailor-made destination for family travel. The kids will be begging to go to theme parks, and teens to celebrity hot spots. Then take 'em to the beaches, where there's carefree frolicking.

Don't Get Caught Short

Some amusement-park rides have minimum-height requirements and/or age requirements. Let younger kids know in advance about possible limitations to avoid disappointment – or tears – standing in front of the cut-out clown with the 'riders must be this tall' requirement. Universal Studios Hollywood and Disneyland® Resort have details in their apps and websites.

FUN ON THE BEACHES

LA's over 20 miles of beaches come in many flavors. Almost all are administered by LA County.
Scan the QR code below to find the right beach for you and your family:

Prams, Strollers & Babies

Most of LA is great for strollers, but if you plan on enjoying the beaches or Griffith Park, child carriers are definitely a better option. Some attractions offer rental strollers. Basics are available in supermarkets and drugstores 24/7, while organics and specialty items can be found at higher-end supermarkets, big-box stores and boutiques. Bathrooms with changing facilities are common, as are family bathrooms.

Dining

High chairs and children's menus are usually available at all casual eateries. Kid-tested menu items are common, so everyone's included.

Free Admission

While museum admission prices for adults can be high, many allow kids in for free.

Child Seats

Children under eight must be buckled up in the car's back seat in a child or infant safety seat; children under two must be in a rear-facing safety seat – reserve one ahead when renting a car.

Accommodations

LA offers every kind of place to stay, from the most famous of luxury addresses to humble hostels near the beach.

Where to Stay if You Love...

☼ Beaches

Santa Monica (p133) has stylish beachfront high-rises; **Venice** (p145) has funky low-rise options, plus some cheapies off the beach; and **Manhattan Beach** (p151) has motel choices both low-key and stylish.

OUR PICK

★

We Love to Stay In...

Los Feliz (p71) This walkable neighborhood is where you'll want to live. Vermont Ave has lovely cafes, great shops and cool places to catch an unusual film. Heading south along Sunset Blvd, you'll probably feel the same way about Silver Lake and Echo Park. These are places to fall in love with friendly, relaxed LA life.

Nightlife

West Hollywood (p121) The Sunset Strip and Santa Monica Blvd have some of LA's most celebrated lounges, bars and clubs. They're also home to some of the region's most stylish hotels.

HOW MUCH FOR A NIGHT IN...

Hostel dorm bed near the beach **from $50**

Midrange double **from $200**

Luxe room at a famous hotel **from $600**

◆ Living the High Life

Beverly Hills (p121) The first, second and third choice for anyone who wants the pampered, luxe life with an overlay of glitz. Five stars are where hotel ratings begin here.

Culture & History

Downtown (p53) LA's compact center is where you'll find top concert halls and art museums. You can walk through decades of history to Chinatown and the Arts District.

Museums & Shopping

Mid-City (p107) Three of LA's top museums are in a cluster on Wilshire Blvd. Stroll up Fairfax Ave to 3rd St, Beverly Blvd and Melrose Ave for the best shopping.

171

Food, Drink & Nightlife

Menu Decoder

Entree Main course. (This is often confusing to non-Americans.)

Split plate Where diners ask the kitchen to divide a plate between two (or more) people; there may be a small surcharge.

Allergies & Intolerances

Travelers with food allergies or dietary restrictions are in luck: LA restaurants are well used to catering to specific dietary needs. Menus often note common allergens in dishes.

?

COULD I HAVE THAT TABLE?

It's an LA thing: no matter how good the first table is that you're offered, you always ask the host/hostess for a different one.

FOOD TRUCK BOUNTY

LA has hundreds of food trucks operating across the city and the region. Some are found in clusters; others operate alone. Some are in the same spot every day; others move around. Sample widely! Many are renowned for their cuisine, especially those serving Mexican food. Consult *lataco.com* for recs.

Martinis & French Toast at a Coffee Shop

In LA (and California), a 'coffee shop' serves coffee, yes, but elsewhere in the USA it would be called a diner or a cafe. Local coffee shops have big menus from breakfast through dinner, many are open late or even 24/7 and some come with full bars.

HOW TO...

Pay the Bill

Ask for the check (or bill) If the place is busy, the check may appear as a suggestion that you move on; otherwise, just ask for it.

Splitting the bill If you want to be fussy about who pays what, tell your server you're splitting the bill when you order; otherwise, if you're just dividing the total equally, you can do that when you pay.

Tipping Compulsory. For bartenders, it's 15% per round or at least $2 per drink; for servers, at least 20% of the check total, unless a gratuity is already included (common for groups of six or more).

PRICE RANGES

The following price ranges refer to the average price for a main course.

$ less than $15
$$ $15–25
$$$ more than $25

OPENING HOURS

Coffee shops
7am to 10pm or later

Fine restaurants
5pm to 10pm

Bars
4pm to 2am

🥂 Going Out
Where to drink

The real question is where not to drink. Like its restaurants, LA has every kind of drinking establishment imaginable. It cherishes its veteran dive bars as much as it holds the stylish 'it lounge' of the moment in high esteem. Pick your mood and neighborhood and you'll find a place. People-watching is always a thing, so tables outside are common.

When to drink Don't delay. The strict 2am closing time means that wandering in at 1am won't make for much of a night. People start early and move through venues with the evening, generally going to darker, louder and moodier places as the hours pass.

Getting in Most places have little or no dress code. You can find swank clubs that care, and they'll let you know they care.

Do I book? If the place is trendy, has a view, has popular music or is otherwise a hot ticket, yes.

HOW MUCH FOR A

Coffee
$3–7

Glass of California wine
$12

Craft beer
$10

Burrito
$12

Non-designer doughnut
$2

California sushi roll
$12

Cup of artisanal ice cream
$6

LGBTQ+ Travelers

While your gaydar will be pinging throughout LA County, the rainbow flag flies highest along Santa Monica Blvd in West Hollywood.

Pride & Celebrations

The festival season kicks off with **WeHo Pride** *(West Hollywood; weho pride.com)* in late May and most of June. As the LGBTQ+ center of Southern California, the celebrations bring huge crowds for its parties, exhibits, shows and parade down Santa Monica Blvd. Amid all the celebrations is a serious political element too, as advocacy and rights issues are core to the community.

Usually a week or two later, in June, **LA Pride** *(lapride.org)* adds the festivities and events with its parade down Hollywood Blvd.

Long Beach Pride *(longbeachpride.com)* has shifted its dates through the years, but look for the parade beginning in May.

Jump to **Halloween** (October 31) and around 500,000 outrageously costumed revelers hit Santa Monica Blvd and its surrounds for spectacular, world-class WeHo fun.

OUR PICK

Open LA

Flashy WeHo gets all the attention for its famous LGBTQ+ scene, but LA is one of the most accepting metro areas on the planet. The entertainment industry and the prevalence of creative types contribute to an open culture that's welcoming from the beach towns to the east.

NITO/SHUTTERSTOCK

BLACK CAT

In 1966, two years before New York's Stonewall Riots, LGBTQ+ protesters stood up to harassment by LA cops at this beloved **Silver Lake bar** (p81), which is still a favorite.

LGBTQ+ TOURS

Starline City Sightseeing Tours has a detailed list of LGBTQ+ sites across LA that can be seen as part of its tours or independently.

Resources

● **Los Angeles Blade** Bills itself as 'Southern California's LGBTQ+ news source.' *losangelesblade.com* ● **The Pride LA** Another good online source of local news and culture. *thepridela.com* ● **WeHo Times** Covers the neighborhood and has good bar reviews. *wehotimes.com*

Health & Safe Travel

Despite its seemingly apocalyptic list of dangers – guns, crime, wildfires, earthquakes – LA is a reasonably safe place to visit.

WILDFIRES

The wildfire season gets ever-longer (at least May through January). Fires limit access to roads and parks, and can cause vacationers and residents to flee for their lives. Fires can quickly overwhelm firefighters and outpace public warnings. If you see the sign of a wildfire, don't wait to be trapped – leave the area.

Insurance

Travel insurance to cover theft, loss and medical problems is essential, especially for international visitors. Domestic visitors should confirm they have proper coverage: injuries or maladies can strike unexpectedly. Trip-cancellation insurance can be a worthwhile expense, too.

International visitors need to have full medical coverage as the costs for any care in the US can be ruinous, or you may be asked for proof of coverage before you are able to receive care.

Stay Informed

Sign up for notifications from LA's Emergency Alert System.

Earthquake!

Earthquakes happen all the time, but most are undetectable. If there's a serious temblor:
- If possible, stay in an open outdoor space.
If indoors, get under a table or stand in a doorway.
- Protect your head and stay clear of anything that might break or fall.
- Don't head for elevators or run into the street.

--- **HOMELESSNESS** ---

Downtown LA continues to be a place where many people live on the streets. It's an ongoing crisis that many find deeply disturbing.

QUICK INFO

Cannabis
Legal in California for medicinal and 21-plus recreational use.

Drink Driving
The blood alcohol limit is 0.08%.

Smoking
Prohibited inside any public space and often outside too.

Responsible Travel

Follow these tips to leave a lighter footprint, support local and have a positive impact on communities.

EV Rental

California car-rental companies have embraced hybrid and electric vehicles. If the price seems high, shop around, as rates change constantly and discounts appear regularly. However, you may find that e-vehicles are among the cheaper offerings because many renters are intimidated by the unfamiliar technology. That said, if you're an EV novice, make sure the company briefs you and makes clear what level of charge is required when you return the vehicle.

Save Precious Water

California's near-permanent drought means that everybody can help save water, including visitors. The state has a list of easy things to do to reduce water use: **saveourwater.com**.

OUR PICK

Help Protect the Beaches

Help the beaches by adopting any trash you see as your own and tossing it. You can do this anywhere in LA!

Drink the Water

There's no need for expensive, brand-name water bottles. Rinse out resealable beverage containers and fill them with tap water (LA's is tasty). One plastic container will last the duration of your trip. If you're given a plastic straw (banned in many parts of LA), rinse, save and reuse. Although restaurants may not immediately give you water when you sit down, it's always available for free.

FROM TOP: LJUPCO SMOKOVSKI/SHUTTERSTOCK, ALENKADR/SHUTTERSTOCK

Resources

- **afdc.energy.gov/fuels/electricity_locations.html** California has thousands of EV charging stations. ● **metro.net/riding/guide/system-maps** Metro system maps are great for planning.

--- **PLASTIC FOR CASH** ---

Look for 'CA CASH REFUND' or 'CA CRV' on beverage containers sold in California (although not wine bottles). Refunds range from 5¢ to 10¢. Find recycling points to collect the cash at *calrecycle.ca.gov*.

Car-Free in LA

Once unthinkable, it's now possible to enjoy a wonderful trip in LA and never need a car. Within California, Amtrak is timely, efficient and often faster than clogged freeways. Metrolink runs commuter trains throughout the SoCal region. In LA, the expanding Metro public transit system combines subways, light rail and buses to cover the city and surroundings. There are stops near many of the most popular sights. Bikes, e-bikes and e-scooters are easily rented in LA, especially at the beaches. The 22-mile **Marvin Braude Bike Trail** (p139) runs along the beaches.

YOUR CARBON FOOTPRINT

Traveling from San Francisco to LA by car emits about 150kg of carbon monoxide; flying, 160kg (per passenger); bus, 20kg; and train, 40kg. Scan this QR code to calculate your trip's footprint:

Climate Change & Travel

It's impossible to ignore the impact we have when traveling; Lonely Planet urges all travelers to engage with their travel carbon footprint, which will mainly come from air travel. While there often isn't an alternative, travelers can look to minimize the number of flights they take, opt for newer aircrafts and use cleaner ground transportation, such as trains. One proposed solution–purchasing carbon offsets–unfortunately does not cancel out the impact of individual flights. While most destinations will depend on air travel for the foreseeable future, for now, pursuing ground–based travel where possible is the best course of action.

The **UN Carbon Offset Calculator** shows how flying impacts a household's emissions.

The **ICAO's carbon emissions calculator** allows visitors to analyse the CO_2 generated by point-to-point journeys.

Accessible Travel

Path to the Surf

Many LA County beaches have beach access accommodations. Six major beaches, including **Venice** (p150), have beach access mats, made from a synthetic mesh that runs from an accessible walkway all the way down to the waterline, allowing people who use wheeled mobility devices freedom to access the beach. *beaches.lacounty.gov/la-county-beach-ada-access*

Hotel Access

Hotels built since 1993 must meet modern accessibility requirements. Major chains usually have rooms adapted for accessibility needs, but it's best to book ahead and double-check they have what you require. Holiday rentals and vintage properties may not be accessible.

OUR PICK

Whether you're visually or hearing impaired or need a break from the frenetic LA pace, LA's beaches are a feast for the senses and offer a more peaceful experience. Find a patch of sand, breathe in the scent of salt air with notes of kelp and let the sound of the surf offer white noise, punctuated by the cries of gulls overhead. Any beach can be a serene escape at the right time, but **Will Rogers State Beach** (p137) has sensory richness and sandy expanses that make it magical year-round.

THE ADA

The **US Department of Justice** enforces the Americans with Disabilities Act (ADA). The act covers many areas, including employment, transportation and accommodations. Details can be found on its comprehensive website. *ada.gov*

Rideshare with a Wheelchair

Rideshare services like Uber offer the option of accessible rides for people with mobility needs. In the Uber app, look for the 'Uber WAV' option when booking your ride.

ACCESSIBLE METRO

In Southern California, Metro trains, stations and buses are all accessible because the system dates from a time after the passage of the ADA. Amtrak requires notice for accessibility service.

Resources

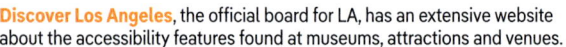

Discover Los Angeles, the official board for LA, has an extensive website about the accessibility features found at museums, attractions and venues.

Nuts & Bolts

Opening Hours

Banks 9:30am-6pm
Monday to Friday, some
9am-2pm Saturday

Bars 4pm-2am daily

Business hours (general)
9am-5pm Monday to Friday

Post offices 9am-5pm
Monday to Friday, some
9am-1pm Saturday

Restaurants 7:30am-
10:30am, 11am-3pm and
5:30pm-10pm daily, some
later Friday and Saturday

Shops 10am-7pm or later
Monday to Saturday,
noon-6pm Sunday; malls
stay open later

Supermarkets
7am-10pm daily

There's no telephone code for LA. All phone numbers have 10 digits.

Tourist Information

Love Beverly Hills Sightseeing, activities, dining
and accommodations information focused on the
Beverly Hills area. *lovebeverlyhills.com*
Discover Los Angeles Comprehensive information on
all aspects of LA. *discoverlosangeles.com*
Visit Santa Monica The coastal city's tourist information
organization. *santamonica.com*
West Hollywood Online info on attractions, accommodations, tours and LGBTQ+ life. *visitwesthollywood.com*

QUICK INFO

Time zone Pacific
Time (GMT/UTC
minus eight hours)
**Country calling
code** 1
**Emergency
number** 911
Population 10 million

ELECTRICITY
120V/60Hz

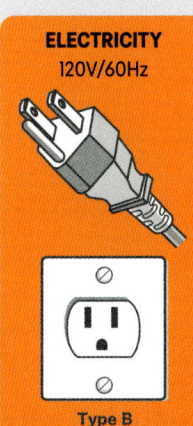

Type B

Public Holidays

On the following
holidays, transportation,
museums and other
services may operate
on a Sunday schedule.
Holidays falling on a
weekend are usually
observed the following
Monday.

New Year's Day January 1

Martin Luther King Jr Day
Third Monday in January

Presidents' Day Third
Monday in February

Cesar Chavez Day
March 31

Memorial Day Last
Monday in May

Independence Day July 4

Labor Day First Monday
in September

**Indigenous Peoples'
Day** Second Monday in
October

Veterans Day November 11

Thanksgiving Day Fourth
Thursday in November

Christmas Day
December 25

Index

Sights p000   **Map pages p000**

1st Street 69
6th Street Viaduct 65
1300 Block of Carroll Avenue 75

A

A-12 airplane 89
Abbey 126
Abbot Kinney Boulevard 151
Academy Awards 29, 48, 57, 62, 113
Academy Museum of Motion Pictures 113
accessible travel 178
accommodations 171
activities 14, 28-9, 46, 137, 139, 150, 151
Ahmanson Theatre 62
air travel 30
Al & Bea's Mexican Food 69
allergies 172
Alto Nido Apartments 43
amusement parks 138, 158-9, 162-7
Anderton Court Shops 125
Angels Point 75
Annenberg Community Beach House 139
architects
  Becket, Welton 48
  Diller Scofidio + Renfro 60
  Gehry, Frank 62, 149
  Gensler 60
  Grosvenor Goodhue, Bertram 57
  Lloyd Wright, Frank 79, 125
  Meier, Richard 130
  Piano, Renzo 113
  Wong, Gin D 125
  Zumthor, Peter 112
architecture 75
  1300 Block of Carroll Avenue 75
  Alto Nido Apartments 43

Anderton Court Shops 125
Avila Adobe 64
Beverly Hills Civic Center 125
Binoculars Building 149
Bob's Big Boy 161
Bradbury Building 63-4
Broad, The 60-1
Capitol Records 48
David Geffen Galleries 112
Eastern Columbia Building 57
Gamble House 99
Getty Center 130-1
Getty Villa 142
Greystone Mansion & Gardens 127
Hollyhock House 79
James Oviatt Building 57
Kirk Douglas Theatre 111
Los Angeles Central Library 57
Los Angeles City Hall 64
Saban Building 113
Samuel Oschin Air and Space Center 89
Security Pacific Building 43
Snow White Cottages 79-80
Union 76 Gas Station 125
arriving in Los Angeles 30
art galleries, *see* museums
Arts District 65
Autry Museum of the American West 77
Avila Adobe 64

B

Baked Potato 160
beaches 16, 137, 143, 150, 151, 170, 178
Bergamot Station Arts Center 139
Beverly Gardens Park 125
Beverly Hills 121-9, **122-3**
  drinking 128-9
  experiences 126-7

film locations 127
food 128
itineraries 124-5, **124**
shopping 129
transportation 121
walking tours 124-5, **124**
Beverly Hills Civic Center 125
Beverly Hills Hotel 126
Beverly Hills sign 125
bicycling 32-3, 126, 139, 177
Biddy Mason Memorial Park 64
Bikes & Hikes LA 126
Biltmore Los Angeles 57
Binoculars Building 149
Blue Ribbon Garden 62
Bob Baker Marionette Theater 102
Bob's Market 75
bookstores 51, 59, 67, 69, 75, 83, 105, 129, 153
Boyle Heights 68-9, **68**
Bradbury Building 63-4
Breed Street Shul Project 69
Broad, The 60-1
Broadway Theatre District 57
Bronson Canyon 76
Bronson Caves 76-7
Bruce's Beach 151
Buna 115
Burbank 155-61, **156-7**
  drinking 161
  experiences 160
  film locations 160, 161
  food 161
  shopping 161
  transportation 155
bus travel 30, 32
business hours 173, 179

C

Cactus Garden 131
California African American Museum (CAAM) 89, 91

California Heritage
  Museum 137
California Science
  Center 89, 90
cannabis 175
Capitol Records 48
car travel 32
car rental 176
carbon emissions 177
celebrities 17, 48, 49, 113, 118, 126,
  127, 129
  Hollywood Museum 45
  Hollywood Walk of Fame 44
Center Theatre Group 62
Cesar Chavez Avenue 69
Chavez Ravine neighborhood 80
Chinese American Museum 59
Cielito Lindo 64
cinemas, see theaters
Clifton's Republic 57
climate 28, 176
climate change 177
Comedy Store 127
concerts, see live music
costs 27, 33, 171, 172-3
Culver Hotel 111
Culver Studios 111
cycling 32-3, 126, 139, 177

D

David Geffen Galleries 112
Davies Guest House 137
DC-8 airliner 89
disabilities, travelers with 178
Disneyland® Resort 162-7, **163**
  Adventureland 165
  Avengers Campus 165
  Cars Land 166
  Disney California Adventure
    Park 165
  Disneyland® Park 162
  Disneyland® Railroad 162
  Downtown Disney District 166
  Fantasyland & Frontierland 164
  Grizzly Peak 165-6
  Hollywood Land 165
  New Orleans Square & Bayou
    Country 164-5
  Pixar Pier 166
  practicalities 166-7
  Star Wars: Galaxy's Edge 162
  Tomorrowland 162-4
Disney's first studio 80

diversity 35
Dodger Stadium 79
Dolby Theatre 48
Dorothy Chandler Pavilion 62
Downtown 53-67, **54-5**
  drinking 67
  experiences 63-5
  film locations 57, 63, 64, 65
  food 66-7
  itineraries 56-7, **56**, 58-9, **58**
  shopping 67
  top experiences 60-1, 62
  transportation 53
  walking tours 56-7, **56**, 58-9, **58**
Dresden Lounge 80
drinking 8, 172, see also Drinking
  subindex, individual
  neighborhoods
  Abbey 126
DTLA, see Downtown

E

earthquakes 175
Eastern Columbia Building 57
eating 6, 172-3, see also Eating
  subindex, individual
  neighborhoods
Echo 80
Echo Park 71-83, **72-3**
  drinking 82
  experiences 79-80
  film locations 75
  food 81-2
  itineraries 74-5, **74**
  shopping 82-3
  top experiences 76-8
  transportation 71
  walking tours 74-5, **74**
Echo Park Lake 75
Echoplex 80
Egyptian Theatre 48
El Capitan Theatre 47-8
El Matador State Beach 143
El Portal 160
El Pueblo de Los Ángeles 64
El Ruso 75
Elysian Park 75
electricity 179
emergencies 175, 179
events 28-9, 48, 165
EV rental 176
Exposition Park 85-93, **86-7**
  drinking 93

experiences 92
food 93
itineraries 88-9, **88**
top experiences 90-1
transportation 85
walking tours 88-9, **88**
Exposition Park 90-1

F

family travel 21, 170
Far East Plaza 59
festivals & events 28-9, 48, 165
film locations 34, see also movie
  paraphernalia, museums,
  individual neighborhoods
film studios 47, 80, 111, 160
film theaters, see theaters
food 6, 172-3, see also Eating
  subindex, individual
  neighborhoods
free experiences 21

G

Galco's Old World Grocery 102
Gamble House 99
gardens, see parks & gardens
Gateway Monument 59
gay travelers 19, 28, 43, 45, 81,
  121, 126, 174
Geffen Contemporary at
  MOCA 63
Getty Center 130-1
Getty Villa 142
Grammy Museum 65-6
Grand Central Market 63
Greystone Mansion
  & Gardens 127
Griffith Observatory 78
Griffith Park, 71-83, **72-3**
  drinking 82
  experiences 79-80
  film locations 76, 78
  food 81-2
  shopping 82-3
  top experiences 76-7, 78
  transportation 71
Griffith Park 76-7
Griffith Park & Southern
  Railroad 76
Groundlings 117

H

Hamburger Mary's 126

Hancock Park 117
Happy Ice 116
Hauser & Wirth 65
Heal the Bay Aquarium 138
health 175
Highland Park 95-105, **97**
  drinking 104
  experiences 101-2
  food 103-4
  shopping 105
  transportation 95
Highland Park Bowl 101-2
highlights 6-21, 44-6, 60-2, 68-9,
  76-8, 90-1, 100, 112-14, 130-1,
  138, 142-3, 151, 158-9, 162-7
hiking 46, 76-7
history 34-5, 43, 46, 47, 48, 49,
  57, 62, 63, 64, 75, 79-80, 89,
  90-1, 125, 137
Hollenbeck Park 69
Hollyhock House 79
Hollywood 39-51, **40-1**
  drinking 51
  experiences 47-9
  film locations 43, 47, 50
  food 50-1
  itineraries 42-3, **42**
  shopping 51
  top experiences 44-5, 46
  transportation 39
  walking tours 42-3, **42**
Hollywood & Vine 43
Hollywood Boulevard 44-5
Hollywood Bowl 47
Hollywood Forever
  Cemetery 48
Hollywood Heritage
  Museum 43
Hollywood Methodist
  Church 43
Hollywood Museum 45
Hollywood Sign 46, 77
Hollywood Walk of Fame 44
Huntington 100

I

Improv, The 117
insurance 175
intolerances 172
Intuit Dome 92
itineraries 22-5, 68-9, **68**,
  see also individual
  neighborhoods

J

James Oviatt Building 57
Japanese American National
  Museum 64-5
Jet Propulsion Laboratory 101
Jim Morrison Mural 149

K

Kirk Douglas Theatre 111
Kohn Gallery 49
Koreatown 107-19, **108-9**
  drinking 119
  experiences 115-17
  food 118
  shopping 119
  transportation 107
Koreatown 116-17

L

La Brea Tar Pits & Museum 115
LA Louver 149
LA Philharmonic 62
LACMA 112
Largo at the Coronet 117
Laugh Factory 127
Leonard Nimoy theater 78
lesbian travelers 19, 28, 43, 45, 81,
  121, 126, 174
LGBTQ+ travelers 19, 28, 43, 45,
  81, 121, 126, 174
Little Ethiopia 115-16
Little Tokyo 64-5
live comedy 117, 127
live music 15, 47, 51, 62, 76, 80, 82,
  104, 127, 150, 160
Long's Family Pastry 59
Los Angeles Central Library 57
Los Angeles City Hall 64
Los Angeles Conservancy's
  walking tours 63
Los Angeles Live Steamers 76
Los Angeles Master Chorale 62
Los Angeles Memorial
  Coliseum 91
Los Angeles Music Center 62
Los Angeles Opera 62
Los Angeles Police Museum 101
Los Feliz 71-83, **72-3**
  drinking 82
  experiences 79-80
  food 81-2
  shopping 82-3
  transportation 71

Los Feliz Theatre 79
Lucas Museum of Narrative
  Art 89

M

Madame Tussauds 49
Malibu 142-3
Malibu Farm Restaurant 142
Malibu Lagoon State Beach 143
Malibu Pier 142
Manhattan Beach 151
Mariachi Plaza 69
Marina Del Rey Parasailing 151
markets
  Bob's Market 75
  Hollywood Farmers' Market 51
  Melrose Trading Post 119
  Original Farmers Market 115
  Quality Seafood 152
  Santa Monica Farmers
    Markets 140
  Silver Lake Farmers Market 83
Mark Taper Forum 62
Martin Luther King Memorial 92
Marvin Braude Bike Trail 139
Melrose Avenue 116
Memorial Coliseum 89
MGM, *see* Sony Pictures
Micky's Weho 126
Mid-City 107-19, **108-9**
  drinking 119
  experiences 115-17
  film locations 111
  food 118
  itineraries 110-11, **110**
  shopping 119
  top experiences 112, 113, 114
  transportation 107
  walking tours 110-11, **110**
Miracle Mile 107-19, **108-9**
  drinking 119
  experiences 115-17
  food 118
  shopping 119
  transportation 107
MOCA 63
money 27, 171, 172-3
monuments 59, 78, 89, 92
movie locations, *see* film
  locations
movie paraphernalia 45, 113,
  114, 161
movie theaters, *see* theaters

Mr Brainwash Art Museum 125
Muscle Beach 150
Museum of Jurassic
  Technology 111
Museum of Social Justice 64
Museum of Tolerance 126-7
museums
  art 60-1, 63, 89, 90, 91, 99, 100,
    101, 112, 125, 130-1, 142
  art galleries 49, 59, 65, 69,
    92, 139
  buildings 99
  film & music 45, 49, 65-6, 89, 113
  history 43, 59, 64-5, 77, 99, 101,
    126-7, 137
  science & nature 76, 89, 90,
    111, 114, 115
music stores 51, 83, 105
Musso & Frank Grill 43, 50

N

Natural History Museum 90, 115
New Beverly Cinema 116
nightlife 116-17, 126, 172-3
NoHo Arts District 160
Norton Simon Museum 99, 101

O

Old Pasadena 99
Olympic Gateway 89
opening hours 173, 179
Original Farmers Market 115
Original Muscle Beach 137
Oscars 29, 48, 57, 62, 113

P

Pacific Park 138
Palace Theatre 57
Palisades Fire 139
Pantages Theatre 48
Paradise Cove 143
Paramount Pictures 47, 160
parking 33
parks & gardens
  Barnsdall Art Park 79
  Beverly Gardens Park 125
  Biddy Mason Memorial Park 64
  Cactus Garden 131
  Echo Park Lake 75
  Elysian Park 75
  Greystone Mansion
    & Gardens 127
  Griffith Park 76-7
  Hollenbeck Park 69

  Huntington gardens 100
  Rose Garden 89
Pasadena 95-105, **96**
  drinking 104
  experiences 101-2
  food 103
  itineraries 98-9, **98**
  shopping 105
  top experiences 100
  transportation 95
  walking tours 98-9, **98**
Pasadena Playhouse 99, 102
Paul Smith 116
Pavilion for Japanese Art 112
Petersen Automotive
  Museum 114
Phoenix Bakery 59
piers 137, 138, 142, 149
Piñata District 18, 65
Pirate's Cove 143
planning
  booking 26, 29
  etiquette 26, 172-3
  itineraries 27
  Los Angeles basics 26-7
  tips 26
Platform 111
Poseidon 139
public holidays 179
public transportation 31-3, 177

R

recycling 177
Regen Projects 49
responsible travel 10, 176-7
rideshare 30, 32
Rodeo Drive 125
rooftop bars & restaurants 50, 51,
    67, 128, 129, 140, 141, 153
Rose Bowl Stadium 99
Rose Garden 89
Roxy Theatre 127

S

Saban Building 113
safe travel 175
Samuel Oschin Air and Space
  Center 89
Samuel Oschin Planetarium 78
Santa Monica 133-41, **134-5**
  drinking 140-1
  experiences 139
  food 140

  itineraries 136-7, **136**
  shopping 141
  top experiences 138
  transportation 133
  walking tours 136-7, **136**
Santa Monica Blvd 126
Santa Monica Farmers
  Markets 10
Santa Monica Pier 137, 138
Santa Monica State Beach 137
Security Pacific Building 43
shopping 12, see also Shopping
  subindex, individual
  neighborhoods
smoking 175
Snow White Cottages 79-80
SoFi Stadium 92
Sony Pictures 111, 160
South Coast Beaches
  145-53, **147**
  drinking 152-3
  food 152
  shopping 153
  top experiences 151
  transportation 145
South LA 85-93, **86-7**
  drinking 93
  experiences 92
  food 93
  transportation 85
sport activities 14, 46, 137, 139,
    150, 151
stadiums
  Dodger Stadium 79
  Intuit Dome 92
  Los Angeles Memorial
    Coliseum 89
  Memorial Coliseum 89
  Rose Bowl Stadium 99
  SoFi Stadium 92
Stories 75
Stories of Cinema galleries 113
subway travel 31-3
surprises 34-5

T

tap water 176
taxi travel 30, 32
TCL Chinese Theatre 44-5
The Broad 60-1
The Improv 117

theaters
Ahmanson Theatre 62
Bob Baker Marionette
Theater 102
Broadway Theatre District 57
Dolby Theatre 48
Dorothy Chandler Pavilion 62
Egyptian Theatre 48
El Capitan Theatre 47-8
El Portal 160
Greek Theatre 76
Kirk Douglas Theatre 111
Leonard Nimoy theater 78
Los Feliz Theatre 79
New Beverly Cinema 116
Palace Theatre 57
Pantages Theatre 48
Pasadena Playhouse 99, 102
TCL Chinese Theatre 44-5
Vista Theater 79
Zombie Joe's Underground
Theatre 160
theme parks 138, 158-9, 162-7
time 27, 179
Time Travel Mart 75
tipping 27, 172
tourist information 179
**Tournament of Roses
Parade 102**
tours 14, 34, 46, 63, 126, 160, 174,
see also walking tours
train travel 30, 31-3
transportation 30, 31-3
trash 176, 177
travel seasons 28-9
Travel Town 76
traveling with kids 21, 170

 U

Union 76 Gas Station 125
Union Station 59
Universal City 155-61, **156-7**
drinking 161
experiences 160
film locations 160, 161
food 161
shopping 161
top experiences 158-9
transportation 155
**Universal Studios Hollywood
158-9, 160**
USC Pacific Asia Museum 99

 V

Vault 114
vegetarian travelers 66, 82,
103-4, 128, 140
Venice 145-53, **146**
drinking 152-3
food 152
itineraries 148-9, **148**
shopping 153
top experiences 151
transportation 145
walking tours 148-9, **148**
Venice Beach Art Walls 149
Venice Boardwalk 150
Venice Canals 149, 151
Venice Pier 149
Venice Reconstituted 149
viewpoints & views 64, 75, 78, 79,
113, 127, 131, 142, 151
Vista Theater 79

 W

walking tours 63, 68-9,
68, *see also individual
neighborhoods*
Walt Disney Concert Hall 62
Warner Bros Studio 160
waste 176, 177
water 176
Watts Towers 92
Watts Towers Art Center 92
weather 28
Webber 939 65
WeHo, *see* West Hollywood
West Hollywood 121-9, **122-3**
drinking 128-9
experiences 126-7
film locations 127
food 128
shopping 129
transportation 121
West Plaza 59
Whisky-a-Go-Go 127
wildfires 139, 175
**Will Rogers State Beach
137, 178**

 Z

**Zombie Joe's Underground
Theatre 160**
Zuma Beach 143

 **Eating**

 A

Ahgassi Gopchang 118
Al & Bea's Mexican Food 69
All Time 82
Alma's Place 93
Artisanal Goods by CAR 103
Asanebo 161

 B

Barney's Beanery 128
Bavel 66-7
Bay Cities Italian Deli & Bakery
140
Belle's 104
Birdie G's 140
Bistro 45 103
Black Cat 81, 174
Bob's Big Boy 161
Buna 115

 C

Café Gratitude 152
Canter's 118
Catch LA 128
Centrico 166
Checker Hall 104
Chili John's 161
Cielito Lindo 64
Clark Street Diner 50
Clifton's 57
Clifton's Republic 57
Cole's 66
Corn Dog Castle 166

 D

Daichan 161
Danbi 118
Dear John's 118
Din Tai Fung 166
Donut Friend 103
Duke's Malibu 142
Dulan's On Crenshaw 93

 E

El Ruso 75
Eggslut 63
Éléphante 140

F
Fair Oaks Pharmacy 103
Felix Trattoria 152
Figaro Bistrot 81
Foster's Freeze 93

 G
Gigo's Cafe 66
Gjusta 152
Grand Central Market 61, 63
Grandmaster Recorders 50
Guelaguetza Restaurant 118

 H
Hamburger Mary's 126
Happy Ice 116
Hello Kitty and Friends Cafe 159
Holey Grail Donuts 140
Hollywood Farmers' Market 51
HomeState 81
House of Pies 81

 J
Joe's Pizza 45
Joss Cuisine 128
Joy 103

 K
Kitchen Mouse Cafe 103-4
Kitchen's Corner 93

 L
Langer's Deli 118
Lard Lad 159
Long's Family Pastry 59
Luv2eat Thai Bistro 50-1

 M
Malibu Farm Restaurant 142
Manhattan Beach Creamery 152
Mariscos El Faro 103
Martha's Hermosa Beach 152
Marugame Monzo 66
Mélisse 140
Mercado La Paloma 91, 93
Mother Wolf 43, 50
Musso & Frank Grill 50
My 2 Cents LA 118

N
Nate'n Al's 128
Nobu Malibu 142

 O
Original Farmers Market 115
Orsa & Winston 66

P
Paradise Cove 143
Paseo 166
Pazzo Gelato 81
Petit Trois 50
Philippe the Original 66
Phoenix Bakery 59
Pine & Crane 81
Pink's Hot Dogs 118
Pizzeria Bianco 66
Playita Mariscos 81
Providence 50

 Q
Quality Seafood 152
Queen St Raw Bar & Grill 104

 R
Randy's Donuts 93
République 118

 S
Salt & Straw 152
Santa Monica Farmers Markets 140
Santa Monica Seafood 140
Scoops 103
Shabu Shabu House 66
Smoke House 161
Somerville 93
Sonoratown 66
Spago 128
Speranza 81-2
Sticky Rice 63
Sugarfish 128
Sunny Blue 140
Superba Food & Bread Hollywood 50
Sushi Gen 66

 T
Tail O' the Pup 128
Teddy's Red Tacos 152
Three Broomsticks restaurant 158
Tower Bar 128
Trejo's Coffee & Donuts 50
Tuning Fork LA 161

 U
Un Solo Sol 69

V
Villa's Tacos 103

 Drinking

1894 104

 A
Akbar 82
Arts District Brewing Co 67

 B
Bar Chloe 141
Bar Flores 82
Bar Lis 51
Bar Next Door 128-9
Be Bright Coffee 119
Black Market Liquor Bar 161
Boomtown Brewery 67
Burgundy Room 51

C
Cabana Cafe 126
Chez Jay 141
Covell 82

D
Dan Sung Sa 119
Divine Vintage 141
Dresden Lounge 80

E
Eightfold Coffee 82
El Carmen 119
EP & LP 129
Ercoles 1101 153
Everson Royce Bar 67

 F
Frolic Room 51

 G
Gold Line 104
Good Housekeeping 104

 H
Harvard & Stone 51
High Rooftop Lounge 153
Highlight Coffee 104

Kumquat Coffee Co 104

Library Alehouse 141
Lock & Key 119
Lodge Room 104
Lucky Baldwin's 104

Micky's Weho 126
Musso & Frank Grill 43

Normandie Club 119

Oga's Cantina 162
Ototo 82

Pam's Coffy 79
Patria Coffee Roasters 93
Penthouse 141
Perch 67
Polo Lounge 126, 129

Rosen Karaoke 119

Simmzy's 153
Snake Pit 119
Stir Crazy 119

Tabula Rasa Bar 51
Tiki-Ti 82
Townhouse & Del Monte
   Speakeasy 153

Velvet Martini Lounge 161
Venice Ale House 152-3

Wally's Beverly Hills 129
Waterfront 153

Shopping

Abbot Kinney Boulevard 151

Amoeba Music 51
Anderton Court Shops 125
Aroyo Records 105
Avalon Vintage 105
Aviator Nation 153

Big Bud Press 105
Book Soup 129
Botanica Olokun 69
Burro 153

Cheese Store 129
Counterpoint 51
Curve 129

Disney's first studio 80
Dover Street Market 67

Edelweiss Chocolates 129

Far East Plaza 59

Galco's Old World Grocery 102
Giant Robot 129
Gold Bug 105
Golf Wang 119
Good Liver 67
Great Labels 141

Hennessey + Ingalls 67
Homage 105

It's a Wrap! 161

Jadis 141
JF Chen 51

Kingswell 83

La Casa del Mariachi 69
Larry Edmunds Bookshop 49
Last Bookstore 67
Lather 105
Lemon Frog 83
Lincoln Boulevard 151

Luxe De Ville 83

Matrushka Construction 83
Melrose Trading Post 119
Mystery Pier Books 129

Neo 39 105
North Figueroa Bookshop 105

Omami Mini 67
On Maritime Records 105
Other Books 69

Paul Smith 116
Platform 111
Pleasure Chest 129
Polkadots & Moonbeams 119
Posers Hollywood 119
Principessa 153
Puzzle Zoo 141

Reverie Bookstand 83
Ripndip 119
Rodeo Drive 125
Row DTLA 67

Santee Alley 67
Shorthand 105
Sick City Records 83
Silver Lake Farmers Market 83
Skylight Books 83
Small World Books 153
Stories 75, 83

Ten Women Gallery 141
Time Travel Mart 75, 82-3

Universal CityWalk 158-9

Venice Skateboarding Stuff 153
Vroman's Bookstore 105

Wacko 82
Women's March Store 69

Send Us Your Feedback

We love to hear from travelers – your comments help make our books better. We read every word, and we guarantee that your feedback goes straight to the authors. Visit lonelyplanet.com/contact to submit your updates and suggestions.

Note: We may edit, reproduce and incorporate your comments in Lonely Planet products such as guidebooks, websites and digital products, so let us know if you are happy to have your name acknowledged. For a copy of our privacy policy visit lonelyplanet.com/legal.

Acknowledgements

Cover photograph: Man cycling on road in front of palm tree under clear sky, Venice Beach, Venice, Los Angeles, California. Haydon Perrier/Kintzing

Back photograph: Nightlife in West Hollywood. Let Go Media/Shutterstock.

THIS BOOK

The 8th edition of Lonely Planet's Los Angeles guidebook was researched and written by Ryan Ver Berkmoes. The previous edition was also written by Ryan Ver Berkmoes. This guidebook was produced by the following:

Destination Editor
Melissa Yeager

Cartographer
Julie Sheridan

Production Editor
Martijn Vos

Image Editor
Hannah Blackie

Coordinating Editor
Sarah Bailey

Cover Researcher
Katelyn Perry

Thanks to
Imogen Bannister, Fergal Condon, Alison Killilea, Kellie Langdon, Anne Mulvaney

Although the authors and Lonely Planet have taken all reasonable care in preparing this book, we make no warranty about the accuracy or completeness of its content and, to the maximum extent permitted, disclaim all liability arising from its use.

Published by Lonely Planet Global Limited
CRN 554153
8th edition – Jan 2026
ISBN 978 1 83869 899 7
© Lonely Planet 2026
10 9 8 7 6 5 4 3 2 1
Printed in China